CREATIVE
NONFICTION™

19

Diversity Dialogues

CREATIVE NONFICTION™ 19

Editor
Lee Gutkind

Managing Editor
Leslie Boltax Aizenman

Business Manager
Patricia Park

Senior Editor
Tracy Ekstrand

Editorial Board
Laurie Graham
Patricia Park
Lea Simonds

Production Manager
Kate W. Radkoff

Online Editor
Jonathan Cook

Editorial Advisory Board
Diane Ackerman
Annie Dillard
Tracy Kidder
Gay Talese

Assistant Editors
Kate Luce Angell
Jessica Mesman

The Creative Nonfiction Foundation gratefully acknowledges the support of the Juliet Lea Hillman Simonds Foundation, Inc., the Pennsylvania Council on the Arts and Susan Ritz.

Address correspondence, unsolicited material, subscription orders and other queries to the Creative Nonfiction Foundation, 5501 Walnut St., Suite 202, Pittsburgh, PA 15232. Telephone: 412-688-0304; fax: 412-683-9173; e-mail: info@creativenonfiction.org; Internet: http://www.creativenonfiction.org. Manuscripts will not be returned unless accompanied by a self-addressed, stamped envelope.

Creative Nonfiction (ISSN #1070-0714) is distributed in the U.S. by Ingram Periodicals Inc., 1240 Heil Quaker Blvd., LaVergne, TN 37068-7000, 800-627-6247; B. DeBoer, Inc., 113 East Center Street, Nutley, NJ 07110, 201-667-9300; Media Solutions, 9632 Madison Blvd., Madison, AL 35758, 615-213-0081. Creative Nonfiction is indexed in the American Humanities Index (Whitston Publishing Company).

Contents

ISBN 1-928645-07-0

9 781928 645078 >

Valuing Differences:
A Message from JPMorgan Chase
William B. Harrison Jr., CEO

JPMorgan Chase is proud to sponsor this edition of Creative Nonfiction, on the importance of valuing differences. This compelling collection of essays reflects our firm's commitment to respect each individual. We recognize that by valuing the unique strengths and experiences that each person brings to the workplace, we become a stronger and smarter organization. I want to particularly acknowledge Walter Shipley, a former chairman of our firm, as the guiding force for this project through his leadership in making diversity an integral part of the way we do business.

These essays feature both established and developing writers, a philosophy that is also very much in line with JPMorgan Chase's global art collection, which provided the image on the cover. The art collection supports emerging artists whose themes often portray social issues. The collage on the cover—"Blue Interior, Morning 1968" by Romare Bearden—is a forceful statement of the African-American experience and more broadly, the human experience.

We hope you enjoy these 16 essays, each reflecting diverse backgrounds, the sharing of a personal event and the challenge of that experience. In a turbulent world, it is the spirit of inclusiveness that brings us together as a global community. Enjoy, reflect and learn.

A Moment of Clarity:
The Story of a Corporate Diversity Pioneer

Lee Gutkind

This issue of Creative Nonfiction began in New York in the summer of 1995. Chemical Bank and Chase Manhattan Bank had agreed to merge. Walter V. Shipley, then CEO of Chemical Bank, was to be the CEO of the new company.

Shipley is imposing—6 feet 8 inches tall—and as John J. Farrell, vice president of human resources at Chase, discovered, he could also be very determined. In addition to the challenges inherent in bringing together a combined workforce of 75,000 employees in 50 countries, Shipley decided that diversity would be a major priority. "Wouldn't it be great to leave the baggage from the two companies at the door and start fresh?" Shipley asked Farrell at one of their first meetings.

With lots of help from Farrell, Shipley outlined plans for a diversity initiative he wanted to launch, beginning with the formation of a council made up of employees from various levels and walks of life, including the highest executive officers. At their next meeting, Farrell produced a list of executives who might serve on the council and a recommendation of one to chair it. Shipley approved the names but then surprised Farrell a second time. "John, my name isn't on this list, and I want to be its chairman."

Diversity initiatives were not uncommon in 1995, and CEOs do participate from time to time. But rarely do they put themselves in the trenches on a regular basis. Even if interested, they don't have time—especially in the throes of a merger. But Shipley intended a dramatic gesture. "There is only one person who can lead the changes in attitude needed here," Shipley told Farrell—and that was Shipley himself.

The Diversity Council first met in February 1996—an event Doug Anderson will never forget. Anderson, an African-American who joined heritage Chase in 1971, was skeptical about the process and the people who would participate, especially Walter Shipley. "There were people in management, both at Chase and Chemical, who had never had any experience with people of color in their entire lives—high school, college or graduate school. They had never interfaced with an African-American in senior management as a peer."

Throughout most of his life, Anderson had always felt like an outsider. He had been adopted at 8 years old, attended a large urban high school, and graduated from an all-black college. He had always been comfortable with himself, but he had never felt as if he were an integrated part of the larger group. Chase had initiated diversity councils before, as had Chemical Bank, but neither had been particularly effective. This time Anderson refused to allow himself to become hopeful, only to be subsequently disappointed.

"I thought to myself, 'I have to find out if Shipley means what he says.'" There were 25 other people in the room—and Shipley was seated beside Anderson. "I looked him right in the eye, and I told him, 'If this is going to be a conversation around nonsense, I don't want to have anything to do with this, because it's a waste of time.'"

Shipley's response changed Anderson's life at Chase Manhattan—and set the tone to change the shape of the entire company. He turned and locked eyes with Anderson. "We're going to learn together about how to get along and work together, and we're going to become a real team," Shipley said.

But Anderson was still not satisfied. The other 25 members of the council were carefully watching this scene. Many shared Anderson's skepticism. Some of the gay members were coming out for the first time, risking their positions and reputations. There was a lot to lose if this man, Walter Shipley, did not mean what he said. "I've been through this before," Anderson told Shipley. "Why is this different?"

Shipley paused and looked around the room. It was a tense moment but crucial for both men. To gain Anderson's trust and cooperation, Shipley had to prove that his intentions were honorable and that his diversity initiative was not a public-relations smoke screen. He turned back to Anderson. "You don't know me. But I am going to tell you something right now. I have made a promise to myself and this company, and I am going to deliver."

By "deliver," Shipley meant, first and foremost, that he intended to set the tone for the entire group by confessing his own prejudices and vulnerabilities—no matter how difficult and revealing. "This," said Anderson, "made a huge difference. That was a moment of clarity for me."

Over the next few months, Shipley's story unfolded. Even though Shipley had gone to a public high school with an ethnically and racially mixed student body, some of his family members held on to the oldest and most demeaning prejudices. "I remember as a kid in high school, playing basketball, and my parents and grandparents cringing when the sweaty towel was passed to me from a black player during a time-out." He came face to face with his own inadequacies at Williams College when he flunked out his junior year. He "screwed up," he said, and felt like a second-class citizen. Later he earned his degree at NYU and was accepted into the training program at the New York Trust Company, and he had nightmares about his failures.

To that point, he blamed himself for his perceived inadequacies; he didn't recognize how entire groups could be alienated and ostracized for no logical reason—until 1959, when New York Trust merged with Chemical Bank. It was really an acquisition, not a merger, and within a year, most of his role models at the bank had either resigned or been dismissed.

The experience became a lesson he would never forget. "I went through the feelings that many minorities must have—that I wasn't quite equal to those who came out of Chemical Bank. And I realized how energy-sapping and value-destroying exclusion could be, as opposed to creating an environment in which everyone feels they have an equal opportunity and there is a positive rather than negative energy force."

This was Walter Shipley's moment of clarity—a moment relived 35 years later in 1995 when Chemical Bank and Chase Manhattan came together and he became the leader of the new corporation. Clarity was reinforced by four daughters, who were confronting the male-oriented culture of the corporate world. His daughters were sometimes denied opportunities and privileges that came more easily to their male peers. "I was embarrassed about not knowing how hard it was for women in business," says Shipley

Not long after the merger, he ran into a female executive based in New York who told him she was being transferred to Europe. "My reaction—I didn't say it—was, 'I wonder how her husband is coping.' Later I realized that if she had been a male executive, I would have never wondered how his wife was coping with the transfer."

The long process of awakening came to a head in 1995. From that point on, Shipley approached diversity with passion, says Farrell. "He was a half-dozen years away from retirement, but it seemed as if he wanted to have some legacy to hang on to, to showcase his career, other than the consolidation of the banks, for which he is known around the world."

Joy Bunson, senior vice president of organizational development at Chase, also was a witness to Anderson's confrontation with Shipley. "Walter insisted that each senior officer formulate similar diversity councils in their own business areas. By getting the senior officers to own the diversity effort, he made it clear to everyone in the organization that the diversity initiative was for real. The senior management team—which was where diversity had to start—got it quick."

Under Shipley's tenure, according to Anderson, the number of minorities in high-level management grew rapidly—from three managing directors in 1995 to 40 in the year 2000. Fred Hill, a former Pennsylvania state trooper who worked his way through law school at the University of Pittsburgh, was recruited from the MacDonald Douglas Corporation as executive vice president of marketing.

"What was interesting to me when I got here, two years after Walter's initiative started, was that there were far more African-Americans and women in senior positions than any other place I have ever worked." Hill became the first African-American appointed to the senior policymaking group for the bank—the policy council. "My appointment was a commitment to diversity on the highest levels of management. My experience, credibility and track record showed that I was qualified for the position, but they were clearly taking a chance on somebody that didn't look like them."

It was Hill whom I first approached with the idea of a special issue of Creative Nonfiction—at a precipitous time, as it turned out. Walter Shipley had recently retired, and Hill, along with William Harrison, the new chairman of the board and chief executive officer, were seeking ways to highlight and honor Shipley's contributions. I met with Hill and Stephen Young, senior vice president of global diversity, yet another appointment resulting from Shipley's efforts. Young coordinates nearly 50 diversity councils involving nearly 1,000 employees at any one time.

The story of how a true appreciation and understanding of diversity evolved at Chase Manhattan Bank is rooted in Walter Shipley's basic decency as a human being, Hill and Young told me, but Shipley and Harrison are also astute businessmen. The mix of races, cultures, ages, religions and orientations that Shipley recognized in the Chase workforce also defined the bank's customers. His decision to make diversity his highest priority was not only the right thing to do, but also good business.

Chase's diversity programs have been cited as a model for other financial institutions, and Farrell, Hill, Young and Harrison are regularly consulted for insight and guidance. Last year Business Ethics Magazine ranked JPMorgan Chase as one of the best 100 corporate citizens, primarily on diversity evaluations, and one of the top 20 gay-friendly public companies in America. In 2001 Catalyst, a nonprofit organization working to advance women in business, gave JPMorgan Chase its Catalyst Award for demonstrating diverse approaches to changing corporate culture.

But establishing an atmosphere reflecting true diversity is an ongoing challenge, especially within an organization that continues to evolve. Recently Chase acquired three companies and merged with J.P. Morgan. Doug Anderson is now optimistic.

"When minorities walk in the door today, their first day on the job, I can look at them in the face and say, 'One day one of you might be our chairman.' When I walked in the door and started my career here 30 years ago, that fantasy never even crossed my mind. Our horizons as minorities are entirely different now from what they were 30 years ago, 10 years ago, and even five years. It began with one man. Walter Shipley made a hell of a difference."

From the Editor
Diversity Dialogues
Lee Gutkind

*W*e are sitting in the Thai Place, a dark, quiet restaurant in the Shadyside section of Pittsburgh, when I clink my water glass with a spoon. None of the other nine people at the table knows why I am clinking my glass.

Three of my grad students in the M.F.A. program at the University of Pittsburgh—Karen Levine, Jessica Mesman and Kathy Tarr—are here with me celebrating Kathy's new teaching assistantship. Joining us are writer Gabe Welsch and photographer Paul Ruby, passing through town on assignment for a magazine. Here too are writer Floyd Skloot and his wife, Beverly, in Pittsburgh visiting their daughter, Rebecca, and son-in-law, Gualtiero, also at the table. Floyd's book, which chronicles his life after being incapacitated by Epstein-Barr virus, will soon be published by the University of Nebraska Press. This is one of his rare cross-country trips; the effort exhausts him and requires weeks of rest and recovery before he can work again.

I have just returned from a meeting at the headquarters of JPMorgan Chase in New York, where the winner of the Walter V. Shipley Award—$10,000 for the best essay on the subject of diversity—was selected. Originally the winner was to be announced in fall 2001, but September 11 and the devastation it caused at Chase have left the project in limbo for months.

If you write for literary journals, as many of the best writers do, you know $10,000 for one essay is an unprecedented sum. It costs less than $10,000 to produce an entire issue of most journals; writers often are paid only in copies. At Creative Nonfiction, we pay $10 a published page—better than most.

Creative Nonfiction received nearly 1,000 entries for the Shipley Award, narrowed down through a painstaking process of reading, evaluation and discussion over many months. Those deemed the best seven were submitted to Mr. Shipley and a half-dozen other executives at JPMorgan Chase who, collectively, would make the final selection of the $10,000-prize winner. Those finalists are published here, anchored with essays by prominent writers commissioned especially for this Diversity Dialogues issue to think and write about the meaning of diversity in the 21st century.

Floyd Skloot is a former actor and marathon runner who, 12 years after the virus attacked his brain, continues to ponder his status as someone whose brain damage relegates him to the category of "disabled." In his essay, "A Measure of Acceptance," which he submitted for the Shipley award, he relates what happens when the government demands he undergo a battery of humiliating tests in order to keep his disabled status—as well as the disability payments that support him and his wife.

Because "A Measure of Acceptance" presents, in Floyd's own words, "an encounter between the disabled and insurance industry in the starkest of lights," Floyd had assumed that Chase, a member of the financial-services industry, might feel implicated "as being part of an industry that is being criticized." Thus, he concluded, his chances of winning the Shipley Award, even though he had been named a finalist, were dim, at best. So when I clinked my glass at the Thai Place that evening, stood up and proposed a toast to Kathy for her teaching assistantship, Floyd thought nothing about it. Even when I brought up the Shipley Award, seemingly as an afterthought, Floyd had no clue, guessing that one of the other people at the table whom he did not know might be the $10,000 winner.

I had not planned this surprise for Floyd, a short, slight man of 54, who walks slowly, with a cane, and seems always cheerful and energetic. But the importance of the coincidence resonated with me: all of these people, including Floyd's wife and daughter, now spontaneously coming together for one night and in one place only a few hours after I had returned from New York, where the contest winner had been selected after more than six months' delay. I was excited, not just to pull off a surprise, but because I couldn't help thinking that it meant something bigger and more far-reaching than just a congratulatory announcement in a restaurant. God knows, Floyd, whose income as a writer has yet to exceed his expenses, could use the money. But what writer or artist, especially those who work with literary magazines, couldn't?

There was something more than all the coincidence and spontaneity here. The fact that an international corporation headquartered in New York would help a small literary journal in Pittsburgh provide a forum for writers from throughout the world to openly discuss and debate racism and prejudice for the sake of promoting diversity was a true gesture and symbol of the coming together of cultures and ideas—a tradition that has enriched our country from the moment of its formation. When JPMorgan Chase, multimillion-dollar sponsors of the Super Bowl, can reach out, recognize and invigorate a highly artful and talented collection of writers, as were all the Shipley finalists, something important is happening, and attention should be paid. A change of mood and of attitude is occurring, albeit slowly and ever so painfully.

So I clinked my glass and said the words. "The Walter V. Shipley Award, $10,000—to Floyd Skloot from Portland, Oregon, a man who has suffered, endured and, remarkably, survived—presented by Creative Nonfiction and JPMorgan Chase." These 10 people—friends, acquaintances and strangers coming together—symbolized a significant moment of diversity and confluence that neither I nor anyone else at the table would soon forget. Some things, tiny magic moments, glow in your mind forever, like stars.

The essays in this issue examine many of the different aspects of diversity, including race, ethnicity, religion, physical and mental disability, species, language, and sexual orientation.

Julia Copeland's "Blindsided" begins with the intriguing first sentence, "Last week I discovered I was black." Jewell Parker Rhodes, in "Mixed-Blood Stew," tells of her mixed-race background and the permeable nature of the color line. Shara McCallum's essay begins with the story of her African/Indian/European/Jewish father and then explores the complexities of being a mixed-race American woman able to "pass." Faith Adiele weaves together her story of growing up biracial, single-parented by a white mother, with her ordination in Thailand as a Buddhist nun.

John Edgar Wideman captures the devastation of hatred that can be spawned by race in "Looking at Emmett Till," which tells of the

14-year-old black youth viciously murdered in the Deep South in 1955 for talking to a white woman. Andrei Codrescu's essay reminds us that the bigotry that fueled that horrendous crime continues to exist today in the "New" South and elsewhere. And Richard Rodriguez takes us on a highly allusive tour of the many meanings of *brown*, raising important questions about the use of English as a tool of the white empire—and about its use by the author himself, a man with "brown thoughts."

Patricia Frisella documents dramatic scenes of violence, terror and discrimination involving a different and widely misunderstood minority—the mentally ill. Eliot Sloan explores gender issues in an attempt to better understand the impact of her father's gay identity on both their lives. Judyth Har-Even recounts an experience familiar to very few of us—that of the Orthodox Jewish divorce ceremony.

Chavawn Kelley, a white Easterner living in Wyoming, tells of being asked to teach writing to her mostly Native-American class using an outdated and disturbingly inappropriate lesson plan. Across the border in Utah, Terry Tempest Williams acquaints us with the Utah prairie dog. The disappearance of this "sentinel of the prairie," she points out, is emblematic of something much larger—the "sixth extinction...that is costing the earth some 30,000 species a year." Human habitats also are disappearing—special, intimate places like Shabilsky's Restaurant in Seattle, Wash., where people of diverse cultures, generations and abilities come together in Kate Small's "Gone in Translation."

On a broader perspective, anthropologist Kurt Schwenk probes the basic question—Why are humans prejudiced against those who are different?—and digs deeply into the foundations of Western knowledge to show that what we have learned and understood about race and diversity is grounded in faulty science. And Francine Prose examines the social phenomenon of "going native"—the adoption of another, often disenfranchised, group's identity, usually by someone from the dominant culture. Prose finds that while going native can be "a matter of colonialism and sexual and cultural exploitation," it also can be part of a life-changing process of self-discovery.

Copeland, Kelley, Har-Even, Sloan, Frisella and Small, along with Skloot, were the finalists for the Shipley Award. We want to thank also all the other entrants to the essay competition and to say how heartening we found it to read so many fine, articulate essays about diversity.

Red, White and Silver

Chavawn Kelley

*T*hree Indian girls sit in the corner of the class-room. Their silver lips burn against their brown skin like the white-hot tips of soldering guns. A boy who dropped out of this school last year has been murdered. His body was found by the side of Sinks Canyon Road about a mile from where the Popo Agie River carries runoff from the Wind River Mountains into a hole below the dolomite cliffs. He was white. The accused are Indian. Now the silver metallic lipstick of the Indian girls warns, "Lay off us."

I am the substitute teacher dressed in the remnants of my former life: black-polka-dot-on-magenta silk blouse, black pleated skirt nearly to my ankles, and leather pumps. The corporate model. My philosophy of substitute teaching: Be nice to the students and they will respond. I pronounce each name carefully. My magenta smile matches my tailored blouse.

"Here's what we'll do today: Read Chapter 2, 'From Opinion to Thesis,' in 'The Lively Art of Writing,' then go to the computer lab so you can begin working on your essays." I sit at the teacher's desk to read the assignment with them. The walls of the room are blank, and the windows are covered by gray springwinter cloud. I crave some note of color or creativity. The disarray of the classroom desks bewilders me. I'll straighten them before fourth period. We read, *The thesis of your essay is your opinion boiled down to one arguable statement.* The author has chosen the topic of silverware to illustrate the essay-writing process.

At home my silver lies in a wooden chest in a cardboard box on a shelf. I brought it with me to this, my new home. We read, *Undoubtedly you can summon up stray observations you have made and bits of information you have heard.* Here, we live in a county larger than New Hampshire or Massachusetts. It includes the Wind River Indian Reservation, the Shoshone National Forest, BLM land out in the Red Desert, and a hundred miles of the Oregon Trail. Cattle outnumber people. On the road, pickup trucks outnumber cars. The nearest mall is a three-hour drive across antelope range. The nearest big city is in another state half a day away, assuming good weather. The teen pregnancy rate, the highest in Wyoming, is equal to that of Los Angeles County. *What these bits and pieces are depends upon your own experience, of course.* Until I moved West, I had never taught in a high school. Never walked in an Indian cemetery. Never watched a powwow.

That first time off the highway four years ago, thorny boughs, serrated leaves and rose hips scraped against the enamel finish of my small city car. On the soft dirt road, the screeching of wild roses excited me in a way that radio at freeway speed never could. My wheels emerged from the thicket onto higher ground. From a fence post shaded by the green of cottonwoods, two magpies flew across the trail. I had never seen birds with such tails weighing back toward earth. They could have been a pair of phoenixes, black with flashes of white, and this some legendary land preserved in autumn. I left my car, its silver trim reflecting back at me, and walked up the hill to the Indian cemetery.

The sons and daughters of the Shoshone nation were buried there. Sacajawea's granite memorial was the tallest. Beside it was one for Jean Baptiste, who had been the papoose on his mother's back. Many of the graves were marked with carved granite, but many more were not. Some of the markers were crosses shaped of native sandstone, the names scripted with black paint on chipping white plaster. The graves were closely spaced, almost a jumble, as if no one need ever rest alone far from his kin. Ancient iron bedsteads stood rusted at the heads and heels of sleeping husbands and wives. Ribbons blew, and five-and-dime whirligigs twirled in the hot August wind. Toys, plastic cars and trucks, faded, stood motionless on the grave of a child, as if he had left them there while he ran off to lunch. Cockleburs hopped rides on my socks, and the stems of tall grasses bowed down as if paying respect, remembering those passed on in other seasons.

The next summer near Crowheart Butte, the yellow moon hung over the dark horizon like a cream soup spoon, slightly tarnished. It looked round and weighted, as if it would crush us if it fell. The pow-wow grounds were open to the night air, and the dancers' footfalls landed on hard-packed earth. The perimeter was sheltered, and electric lights lit a rush of color. I sat huddled in my fleece jacket on the bleachers. Cold nights, the first week in June. I would know to bring a blanket next time. Behind me the thick aroma of Indian fry bread floated from a dimpled silver concession truck, and children lined up at its window, anticipating the taste of that hot, wonderful smell in their mouths and the fullness of it in their stomachs.

Men sat in lawn chairs around a drum and beat the rhythm of the dances. Wives and grandmothers sat behind them. The different drumming groups encircled the ring, and the drumming moved from one drum to the next. Dancers danced. They wore numbers like the ones I used to pin to my shirt when I ran the Peachtree Road Race. Male traditional dancers wore eagle-feather bustles tied to their waists. Fancy dancers wore them on their shoulders and arms, as well. One young man had tied iridescent silver CDs to his bustles. Men and women carried eagle feathers in straight fans with beaded handles. The female jingle dancers wore sheaths adorned with the lids of Copenhagen chewing tobacco cans twisted into cones. The silver jingles clicked together as they moved to the drumbeats.

I love to dance. I would have loved to dance at the powwow. But I watched. There is a dance I could have danced. Everyone, male and female of all origins and ages, is invited to dance in the intertribal dance. I could have danced that dance, but I watched.

Just be certain that you have in mind absolutely everything you know about silverware. Pieces in my silver pattern include jelly server, butter spreader, cream sauce ladle, sugar shell, cold meat fork, lemon fork, pickle fork and bonbon spoon. I have the butter knife, the sugar shell and six place settings of dinner knives, dinner forks and salad forks, teaspoons and soup spoons. The murder was execution-style, with a shot to the head.

Until I moved West, I had never watched a powwow. Never seen a Fourth of July parade. Never slept in a hospital bed.

On the Fourth of July, the great-great-granddaughters of Chief Washakie paraded astride the finest animals, their saddles decorated with beaded roundels of the wild rose, symbol of the Shoshone tribe. They wore their ceremonial dress. Soft, fringed elk hide and deerskin, intricate beadwork, feathers. On a flatbed trailer covered with Indian blankets and collected sage, the Clark Trumbell Drum Group and

Singers joined Josephine Redman, 89-year-old parade marshal from the Northern Arapahoe tribe. Shoshone and Arapaho veterans in their Army, Navy and Marine uniforms, long braids, sunglasses and solemn feather bonnets, carried the American and Wyoming flags. The entire length of Main Street was crowded with citizens, young and old, Indian and white, and they all raised their hands to their hearts as the flags passed by.

Fire engines blasted and antique cars tooted. Children rushed forward to grab at candy flung into the street. A steady stream of cowboy hats, wagons, buggies and horses passed. My friend Harvey drove a red and green stagecoach pulled by a team of great, blond Belgian draft horses. At one end of the "Education Yesterday and Today" float, the school marm rang a bell while the prairie children waved their little blackboards. At the other end, students sat at desks topped with retired computers. The Indian students were absent.

Look over your inventory and ask yourself questions. You might come up with something like this: A. I wonder why some silverware is heavier than other silverware. B. What's the meaning of the expression, "born with a silver spoon in his mouth"? C. Why do so many women want to own sterling silver? Why are we reading this? I turn to the front of the battered paperback. Copyright 1965. Almost 30 years ago. I am the substitute teacher. Tell them to stop reading. I don't tell them to stop.

Our Fourth of July rodeo is the longest-running annual paid rodeo in the country. Over a hundred years. One of the events is the wild horse race. I watched from the stands as a jumble of cowboys and bareback horses sorted themselves out, as each horse was subdued, saddled and mounted. Two particularly rowdy horses bucked and circled, confounding the remaining pair of cowboys. "Those must be Indian ponies!" the announcer howled over the public address system, his joke no compliment. "Those must be *white* ponies," the Indian man behind me muttered.

That night, explosions of fireworks punched the sky, and everyone seemed to go home satisfied, but today in this school, the Indian girls wear war paint on their voiceless mouths.

Some of the Indian parents are keeping their kids out of school, and many are threatening to withdraw their sons and daughters. Enroll them in the high school on the reservation. The whites are after the Indians again.

My friend Janie, who teaches math and algebra, is angry, too. She's having to do her regular work many times over by writing out the makeup assignments and grading them separately while defiant Indian men-boys—some of them her students—are sitting out on the stone wall in front of the school, smoking cigarettes. And when she drove by South Elementary on her way home for lunch, she saw them shooting baskets into the too-low nets.

Last night I dreamed No Hall Passes. Everybody just stay in your proper classes, and everything will be all right. No. Murder has broken the usual order, and silver lips speak our differences. What is the difference between a clear soup spoon and a cream soup spoon? A clear soup spoon is the same as a tablespoon. A cream soup spoon is perfectly round.

Look for relationships. Why do so many women want to own sterling silver? With the same amount of money a woman could buy a great many beautiful things. But she chooses to buy silver. She may even make real sacrifices to buy it.

My pattern is "18th Century," introduced in 1971 when I was a girl and my mother had a subscription to House Beautiful, where it was advertised. The design is simple: The handles are fluted, flaring into scallops at the end. When I was 22 and defining life on my own, I joined the Silver Club at Rich's department store. For the pleasure of setting the pieces in their proper places on my unsteady table, I made monthly payments from my entry-level salary.

Obviously we tend to connect silver with riches. That silver spoon probably came down to us from an era when only kings and queens and noblemen could afford to own real silver.

Later I worked in a stylish silver building. A tall silver building in suburban Atlanta's Perimeter Center. The windows didn't open. The oil embargo had dictated the Btu of the air-conditioning system without forecasting the heat of hundreds of humming business machines. By afternoon, clouds of smoke obscured the acoustic ceiling as programmers linked lines of computer code while dragging at chains of cigarettes. The dark doors to the halls remained closed and locked for security.

Many days at lunch I changed out of my leather pumps and put on socks and my old running shoes. I fled to the remnant woods behind the building to eat by a small creek. There water striders strutted across pools that flowed over the bellies of water-smoothed rocks. I admired the sunlit rings that formed where their filament legs made contact with the water's surface. In the fall a tulip poplar dropped her yellow skirt to the ground and raised her bare limbs to the sky, and I wanted to do the same. The fragrance of overripe grapes from a scabby muscadine vine shouted, "Come drink my wine!" But I couldn't. I had to get back.

Can it be that silverware is a status symbol?

In my cubicle hung the Western Wilderness calendar. For months I kept that mountain scene from the Wind River Indian Reservation up on my wall. That blue granite mountain and violet lake. When thunderstorms built to violent force outside, I left my cube to stand at the curved windows and stare with my co-workers as shields of water clattered to the parking lot and coddled landscaping below.

During those years, I made monthly payments on the one new car I've ever owned. After work I waited at traffic lights with the air conditioner blowing air that smelled of engine exhaust and Freon. From tall aluminum poles, lusterless arrows and discs directed four lanes of cross traffic and four lanes of left turns. My nylon pantyhose and cotton underwear wore the wetness of waiting, and wrinkles set into my skirt and blouse as if by steam pressers.

So silver is a symbol of wealth, security, superiority.

My first summer in Wyoming, after the powwow in Crowheart and a weekend of camping in the Tetons, on an empty highway 15 minutes from home, my last thought was, "That car isn't going to stop." I saw his face, empty as a bottle. I didn't want to believe in alcoholism on the Rez. By bloodline and years, he was an elder. I didn't know government checks were issued on the first of the month. By blood alcohol, a stereotype. The one new car I have ever owned.

So beautiful were the blue-greens of the evening light, the greenness of the reservation's pasture land, the deepening umber of the mountains, and the cool scent of the air as I waited for the siren. For weeks those shifting colors spread across my hip, and diamonds of windshield glass sprung forth around me. I'd strewn Highway 287 with them. They skittered across clean hospital tile. They appeared as if from the hinges of my joints, from the spirals of my hair, as manifestations of sharp thoughts. I still keep a few in a black lacquer box my father brought me from China.

A boy who dropped out of this school last year has been murdered. His body was found about a mile from where the river carries runoff from the Wind River Mountains into a hole below the dolomite cliffs. I am white. The accused are Indian.

And no matter which position you take, you must be able to defend it. That, after all, is the whole purpose of your essay—to defend your thesis.

The Indian girls wear silver lipstick. They read in the corner without comment or question. What do they make of these silver spoons? In school there is talk of drugs in connection with the murder. Does methamphetamine make all boys king?

Now you are uneasily aware that a rigid either/or position would be almost impossible to defend. So you must take one more step. Since you cannot possibly prove that sterling silver is always a status symbol, you must indicate the degree of truth in your thesis and, if possible, the circumstances under which you are considering it.

I've read that eagles are the messengers of heaven. They fly high and see all the goings on of the world below. Because of the virtues associated with the bird—strength, speed, freedom, aerial grace and hunting skills—their feathers represent honor and are highly valued. Feathers are given as gifts or granted in response to some act of discipline or humanity or to members of the armed forces for valor. The feathers represent the wearer's virtues or an acknowledgment of his achievements.

Carrying a fan of eagle feathers is like holding the hand of a guide. Were a dancer to drop an eagle feather, he would not pick it up. A special, highly esteemed person would be called to make a prayer as part of returning the feather to its owner.

Your arguments might run something like this: Thesis A: The average housewife seldom uses her sterling silver. She "shows it off" exactly as her husband "shows off" his expensive new car—to impress their friends. Thesis B: The average housewife needs to surround herself with as many beautiful things as possible. Otherwise she is likely to find her life drab and meaningless. Far from being a mere status symbol, sterling silver is an intimate and enduring symbol of basic family relationships.

Mother's pattern is "Royal Danish." The handle is fluted, but instead of flaring at the end, it has the openwork pattern of a crown. One time when I was 10, I dropped one of Mother's teaspoons down the garbage disposal. A dozen years later, I took that spoon to a silver repair service. They smoothed out the torn and bitten edges, and like a finger dipped in wax, it looks as if they dipped it in molten silver, but it was never really fixed. No one knows much about the murder.

After having considered both sides, you will settle eventually on the view that seems to you to be closest to the truth.

"I forgot my disk. Can I go to my locker and get my story?"

"Okay, then meet us at the computer lab." My philosophy of substitute teaching: Be nice to the students and they will respond.

So always look very closely and objectively at views opposed to your own. If you do this, you may be forced to concede a point here and there, to qualify your thesis a little more strictly — but this merely leads to greater accuracy in presenting your own view.

The classroom revives with low whispers and movement of papers. After a few minutes, I go out with the class, turn off the lights, and lock the door. Do I make pleasant conversation with them in the hallway? Not really. We head down to the computer lab. Did that one make it back? Or the one who had to go to the restroom? Was he one of the ones who answered a hip "Yo" when I called his name from the roll? The heels of my shoes clack on the linoleum. I wish I'd worn something else.

In the computer lab I sit in one of the empty chairs between two dark-haired girls, one Indian, one not. Both sit in front of blank computer screens.

"I can't think of anything to write," says one.

"Write about anything you have an opinion on, anything you feel strongly about," I coax.

"Can I write about my friend who was killed?"

The girl looks down into her lap and then up at the screen.

"Yeah, you can write about that."

I turn to the girl on the other side. "What are you writing about?"

"Nothing."

"Well, you must have an opinion on something. What do you like? What do you do?"

No response.

"Your jacket is from the Intertribal Powwow in South Dakota. Do you dance? Could you write about that?"

"No."

And then you are in a stronger position than ever to write your essay. You can defend your thesis with real conviction.

The bell rings and I look around. Only about a third of the class is left. The two girls. A pair of lovebirds who, to their credit, have been working on their essays. Some others. I wasn't watching the doors. They've all snuck out.

I've dropped a teaspoon down the garbage disposal.

I don't know how to pick up a feather that has fallen.

I don't have a thesis.

*With this essay, **Chavawn Kelley** completes a trilogy set in Wyoming's Wind River country. The first of the three, "Why I Love the Dump," appeared in Northern Lights and was honored as a Notable Essay in "The Best American Essays 1997." The second, "There Is No Such Thing As a Perfect Vacuum," was awarded the Wyoming Arts Council's Frank Nelson Doubleday Award. Kelley is also the recipient of the 2001 Wyoming Arts Council's fellowship for nonfiction. She lives in Laramie, Wyo.*

The Green Room

Eliot Sloan

*L*ayla and I are 14. Her lipstick is a hard, red line.
We sit on rock and watch the waves, and on the other side, New Jersey:
lit signs and factories. If I close my eyes, our world is just this, signs
on the horizon. But we dream that this is the ocean, and we can also,
if we try, think pure thoughts of loving and family. We talk here in
this place on the pier by the river with New Jersey on the other side.

"I am afraid I will not say goodbye to my father before he dies,"
she says.

"I am afraid that my father will get sick and won't tell me," I say.

The night breathes images, smiling fathers and lost fathers. I wonder
if God will come down here tonight, if God knows this place. The
night becomes colder, and we are tired. We would like to sit on this
cold shore, sinking in sand, and watch the sun lift the sky in color.
But here it is dark and shivering, and the colors of night change as we
become very young just by looking, and we need each other and the
right father to last.

My father left my mother for a man. She found love letters that
he and another father sent back and forth for years while she was
sending me off to school, cooking dinner, searching for his missing
scarf or pen. She could not find for him what he was missing.

A freckled girl my age named Lizzie told me in the fourth grade.
Her mother had been gossiping about my father, and Lizzie overheard.
At 9 years old, my hair hung in two brown, lumpy braids, and I was
beginning to need glasses to make out the dry sentences in science-
class filmstrips. Her hot, sugary breath on my face as she pulled me
behind some army-green lockers. "Your dad's *gay*," she said. Just like

that, no introductions. "My mom said so." The word sounded ominous, foreign, exotic, and I'm sure neither of us knew its meaning. Then she smiled, and I studied her tiny rows of even teeth, how one attached so cleanly to the next.

Weeks of family meetings started, with my father giving all kinds of vague answers, saying life was "neither black nor white, Sweetheart —it's complicated" and my mother glaring at his fumbling speech from the sofa across the room.

My father told me when I turned 11 that he loved the taut, bronzed, male body, its rippled strengths and deepest voices. I imagined his dreaming of the powerful grip on his shoulder, the stubbled face at his height, leather jackets and big, white teeth. My father is in love with men, their voices and scents. He says he has always desired them but was too afraid. I had to repeat it over and over and over: My father is a gay man. My father is a gay man. He is also my father.

I met his men over breakfast. They were there to greet me when I woke up, eager to win me over with complicated eggs or a bike ride in the park. They were large and sometimes hairy, and I confused their names. My father was protective, calling me "Baby" and "Princess," stroking my hair.

It was an understanding we had, my father and I, that I would not tell my mother about the loud party he took me to, where I at 13 was the only female in a three-level house, or the stack of male magazines I found under the table near his bed. At my mother's house, my life was all about homework and dinner on time. I told her only of the way he'd learned to braid my hair almost as well as she did.

It is January, still hot here in Arizona, and I've just had my 28th birthday. An oversized prickly pear cactus crawls into my window, and the stars out here in the desert are fatter and more brilliant than any I've ever seen. I'm lying on my bed, looking out at them when the phone rings once, twice. It is Layla, crying, calling to say that she just found out that her dead father had been gay and died of AIDS, and she never knew. Back in 1985, the doctors had told her family he had meningitis. I remember he was quarantined so that she and her brother couldn't even touch him or share his food in his last months.

It's been six years since I've heard her, the breaths taken and those held, the memory of her enormous lips stretched into a smile after something I'd said. At 13 we lay up in her loft bed one night and talked about praying: how she asked God to save her dying father, how I squeezed my eyes shut and hoped that someone would come down to this tiny hole of an apartment and save her, Layla.

I came to sleep over that Saturday night wearing a knitted, purple vest my grandmother had given me, a knapsack under my arm. Her father was tall and edgy and didn't seem sick, fixing salad with a sesame dressing, tahini hidden inside. Her mother, a former ballerina and model, took a long bath, and clouds of steam spiraled from under her toweled, dark hair as she joined us at dinner. It all seemed so exotic to me—the father cooking, the mother a dancer, a loft, the talks of God.

Back in that deep night while we prayed, clutching each other, her small breasts were hard against my chest, our thin, pink nightgowns holding in loosely all that our bodies wanted to show. She smelled like garlic and cherries and something faint and other, a light coating on her skin of sweat, maybe fear, keeping me warm as we curled together. The patterns of her parents' muffled whispers in the next room seeped into my dreams that night, tangled voices.

That year, in eighth grade, I took a photography class, and she was my subject. I photographed her while she slept sometimes in the early weekend mornings, hoping I could take just a tiny bit of that beauty for myself. I looked at her legs, wrists, snapping away as sunlight slanted her body, the gray sheet cutting soft diagonals across her pale skin, birthmarks like tiny wounds. Snow on the hushed streets outside and the smell of coffee from the kitchen. I seemed always dark next to her, shadowed. Men looked at her on the street, even when she was 14. Women looked at her. I looked at her. She showed me everything, too much some days, so I had to tell her to stop. Laughing, I'd cover my eyes and peek through the fingers.

We walked across the small, frozen boat pond in Central Park at Christmas holding mittened hands, her breath curling into flower shapes, lights twinkling in the windows on the West Side and music in our heads, the same song. We sang at the top of our lungs, chasing each other across the ice, slipping, racing to the Alice in Wonderland statue to climb up her hair in the fading daylight while both of our mothers must have been at home lying alone curled up in a ball against the cold on those nights of longing.

I used to ask her over and over: Am I a woman or a man? I would feel fragile sometimes, unsure because I have a boy's name, and sometimes she'd pretend I was a boy when we'd practice kissing. She said she had to pretend in order to teach me. I told her I knew about women, what's inside them: a green room like the underneath part of a wave, walls of emerald velvet coiled against the chaos of air and light. If someone really looked and shone a light deeper, I whispered, her eyes so close I could see the blue specks around her pupils, they'd see that in my green room, I was really a man. A father of sorts. Something maybe evil.

I am 13. My father and I agonize because there is a school function next week, an auction and a parent-teacher meeting. He wants to bring his live-in boyfriend. I am horrified. "What is it?" he says to me softly as we put out cheese and crackers for his lover in the next room. "What about that time he took you to see a play last month? Don't you love me and the person I love?"

"You are unfair," I say under my breath. "Not like other dads," and we go back and forth like this until the cheese knife slips into my thumb, and I bleed onto the scratched Formica kitchen counter.

My dad's friend dies of AIDS. My father calls me in tears and tells me to put on a dress, to hurry up, we're going to his funeral in Queens. I have been studying the disease in biology class, and when the teacher asks what we know of it, I fiddle with my bracelet, busy myself drawing circles in the margin.

At home I am under the covers calling Gay Men's Health Crisis to see if I could have gotten it from the time his friend shared my fork last summer, and what about when he used the shower? I am terrified; we know nothing. My father tells me he is healthy, not to worry, but I don't believe.

The way it seems to me, all of my friends' fathers are out playing ball with them in the park on Sundays, hugging their moms in the video store on Lexington and 80th. I long for a different father, one who's normal and shares Cheerios instead of caviar, Muppet movies instead of tormented French films, love stories about girlfriends instead of boyfriends. I must be the only kid like me in the whole world, I think to myself. "I will never tell," I chant over and over like a mantra as I fall asleep.

But there is also this: It is dark already outside on a late Sunday afternoon as I wake up warm after a nap on the sofa with him, its wine-dark velvet pressing a pattern into my cheek. My father lights candles as we listen to opera. He wears a thick, white robe over his clothes so I can see the long, curled, dark and gray hair on his chest. It feels as if we are alone in this world, the water of the music spilling through my hair, my father grabbing my hand and stroking the fingers. He tells me how he can see the lines on his father's face at night in his dreams. I butter dark pumpernickel bread in fat slices for him, open his beer and take a sip, dream of a boy wanting to touch me, to run his hands over me, and I shiver to myself in the dim light. Boys' hands seem impossible; why would they want to touch me? I am scrawny still, all angles and sharp places.

My father tells me as we walk the dog one night that I am an extension of him, that we are hardly different at all. His decision to be with men makes me feel ugly, barren, rejected. I look into the mirror and pull the hair over my eyes until I can't see his face anymore.

His boyfriends fuss over me as if I'm a diva, buying me Hermès scarves though I'm only in eighth grade, teaching me how to make a martini. They share a part of my father that I will never touch, but I know that I have what they really want: I have his heart.

Afternoons in the gathering dusk I walk to the Met alone through pinkish snowlight swirling around my scarf and lashes. I look at the paintings by Van Gogh and dream of summer, the taste of raspberries and scratches on my arms from crawling through bushes. In contrast this city seems to me the place of the black, brittle, burned parts in the heart. But cities also hold some kind of anonymity. I can lose myself.

I wander home, and Dad and I eat together late. He drinks wine and talks to me about love. He tells me he believes in different kinds of love, that there is the "passionate" kind and the "settling" kind. He makes reference to some trip he took down the California coast with the top down and the ocean breezes whipping the cypress trees, the smell of eucalyptus in the air, a lover at his side. He won't tell me the name of this person. I do the math and know he was married to my mother at that time. My face turns hot, red. I ask him to tell me. He says, "When you're 18, maybe." Just like that. And he walks away, down the hall to his room. I try to swallow my tears like an awful, thick pill. I think of his friend whose funeral I attended, and I imagine that someday I could lose my father, our paper-reading breakfasts and running with him in the park, the pounding sounds of his breathing, racing him, my father, our legs after the other, one, two, Sunday light on the reservoir measuring our pace—"Come on, Honeybunch, slow down for your dad," he says—and I feel better and smile and turn around, running, running, around and around.

I have tried to understand how he felt. I have tried to write about my father.

On Saturday mornings—their only time together now—when he woke up and saw her next to him, he was instantly filled with that old mixture of familiarity, repulsion, regret and emptiness, all at once. Then immediately after, like clockwork, he'd think of their child in the next room. Weak sun angles would slant in the window in dusty streams pathetically trying to warm the unforgiving concrete on the quiet streets outside, an occasional snow flurry turning the streets a hushed gray. He shivered, thinking of having to move his car in an hour and yet the relief of leaving these thin walls of guilt, betrayal, her angry tears bitter as the tiny bowl of ever-present, overcooked greens on the table at Passover, the child's brown, liquid eyes—all these things made the short walk over icy patches, over the crunch of salted streets under his boots, even past the few panhandlers, blue and desperate on Park Avenue so early on a quiet morning shaking their cups, seem a relief. Maybe today he'd take the child, his child, bundle her up in her red, wool coat, her mittens that clipped on, her teeth chattering as she ran out the door of their apartment building holding his hand tightly, tripping, breathless, past the silent, stony doorman in his cheap, green coat with the number of their building emblazoned over his heart. Her hand in his so small and strong—every time it had the power to amaze him. Her total trust and loyalty. Was she able to look past what she saw in his face, the patches of truth and lies and the stinging, to forgive him, or did she just see and trust the outside layer? Hours on a therapist's leather couch still could not provide the answer only she could give.

He looked over at his wife asleep next to him. Incredible how she could sleep through anything at all, curled into a ball against his back, her fingers often in tiny fists. She could sleep through even this between them now, these battles and the imminent end, her blond hair spread like a yellow fan across the pillow covered in now-faded chintz sprinkled in an abstract, gold-and-green design. He dreaded the moment when she'd open her eyes and look at him. He dreaded their blue and that early crack in her voice as she asked for water or another blanket or his arms around her.

He sat up and stared out at the Christmas trees on Park Avenue. It must be early; their jewelry of tiny, white lights still formed a perfect line south toward the Pan Am Building. A light snow fell. As she'd sleep through the hours, he was used to staying quiet in the room like this, sometimes awake the whole night. Other times he'd pace and check on the child—her breathing—an old ritual now he couldn't let go of, though she could get herself to school alone now, and he knew how silly it was to worry about that perfect, simple in-out of her small chest, her violet-veined lids thin as wings flickering slightly in the faint glow of the street lights from the window, her fingers clenched around her orange, patterned baby quilt that she refused to give up. He would stalk the shadows in the apartment, drink some wine to try to slow his thoughts.

He'd met his wife 17 years earlier at a big Midwestern university—both from Brooklyn and both fleeing their loud, abrasive, Jewish upbringings for a gentler, nasal accent; for an airplane trip too frightening for either of their neurotic mothers to venture; for a cold so intense, so raw and biting that it made you feel your real bones, your real edges, no padding to soften its blow. She was 17, too thin and blond, her lipstick on strong and her laughter ringing out over the lake from a boat the first time he saw her that lazy afternoon. He was fuzzy from a drink still in his hand as he walked down the lawn in back of his fraternity to watch the boats and the sky and the long strips of cloud beyond the trees. Living there then had made him notice things like trees and clouds, a line of Shakespeare, the smell of a storm. He'd forgotten how to do that now. The child seemed to have that, though, the ability to smell and see. He wanted to say to her, "It will hurt you; try to ignore it. Feeling too much will only sting." But he'd look at her tiny face and say nothing, hoping she'd understand on her own.

The first time he heard that laugh across the lake, it felt like a home. It made him remember drinking tall glasses of cold beer with his father on steamy, August nights and sharing a cigar. He thought of the smell of the Atlantic and the crash of the waves on Labor Day, his mother's long, salmon-pink, silk scarf she wore to parties to look dramatic and the faint notes of his favorite Mozart aria pattered in his brain. That laugh brought back the times before his father's coughing and slow death from cancer. "Too sensitive," his mother had always said to him in a nasty tone, "It'll hurt you in the long run if you don't toughen up."

Tough. *That was the word his mother used, friends used, the word he was not and tried to be and the word that seemed to matter the most. She'd shriek it at him as he cut strawberries at the bakery after school, his head barely reaching the counter, slicing each blood-colored ruby into quarters, eighths, rounds, his mother's hair a web-like mass of blond and auburn — whatever the color of the season — her clothes garish and provocative, bright silks and satins even on an ordinary, November day, his father silent and smoking in his apron behind the bakery door, blanketed always in a light dusting of flour.*

He'd been embarrassed by his father then, thought him uncultured, unsophisticated, common — and his mother glamorous and worldly, seductive — but now he saw her sharp edges and narrowing eyes. He could remember now how she'd slap his face after her second vodka of the evening, yelling out words that made no sense in a garbled stream of fury and frustration. She'd refuse to speak to him for days and play stormy sonatas on their baby grand. She gave birth to his sister when he was 9 and handed her over to him simply, a small bundle of red and pink and tears and needs, into his arms. His mother loved the opera, Proust, dancing, lavish trips to Cuba where men gave her corsages and carried her bags, her husband a dark shadow somewhere hovering behind her. But he knew his mother felt at least the thrill of a box seat on the snowy opening night of "La Boheme," the twinkle of champagne running down into her toes and the smell of fresh flowers in spring — she devoured the rich charge of headlines and news in the Sunday Times, understood his passion for politics, for power, for prestige. After a week of drinking and throwing shoes at him, she'd come home carrying three new, expensive, light-wool suits from Lord & Taylor, a silk tie to match, cufflinks shining in a velvet box. She knew he loved to look expensive, to feel smooth, new fabrics against his skin as he rode the subway to law school and dreamed of having lunch at the White House with JFK. She understood his love of travel, of good restaurants with linen cloths and hushed waiters. His father had seemed so tired, so pale, the last bastion of old Russia, his steps too slow, his accent too heavy, the flour caked under his nails humiliating.

Her laugh across the lake hit him instantly, and he had to meet her. She was even better than her laugh — tall, graceful, no trace of accent, her eyes a clear, turquoise blue. She looked like a shiksa, and he loved that. She looked like his future. So when law school arrived on time, and he began plugging through it like wading through choppy water, the question of marriage came up so easily he didn't even remember proposing. He could already see them laughing over gin-and-tonics as the summer breeze hit them on the ferry to Nantucket; he could imagine them at Christmas parties once he became partner—her in some long, blue, velvet dress and smelling like Chanel and his tuxedo dark and crisp against her pale arm; he could see children in the best schools and camps and at home with a nanny before bed—and he knew that she too wanted all this. He loved to dance and needed that rhythm, that sway of damp bodies against his own and its pulse, but he figured she'd learn that in time. He'd felt so ignorant back then, so naive when he first met her. She'd had tons of boyfriends and moved faster than he did, making him feel awkward and too slow. Her passion frightened him—it still did—a raw lust emanating from her like light that he hadn't expected in such a refined, cool, sleek girl. She'd engulf him with total abandon, and he wouldn't know what to do, how to respond. Usually he felt a kind of tenderness but nothing else, only that vast wall with his mother's voice echoing through the cracks, telling him to be tougher, faster.

Amazing how he understood pain now in such a vaster, deeper way, as if he held it in his pores and muscles and bones. When they'd met at college, all they did was laugh and drink and go sledding and then laugh some more. No pain, no memory, no decisions or stress or practical worries that he sensed his young daughter already carried on her shoulders like a yoke. No, only impatience for when they could buy a cottage in Southampton, or difficulty deciding between the green or the pink dress in Palm Beach, which tie to wear to the dinner with the partners at the firm, which nursery school to send their daughter to, where the best club to learn tennis was. Laughter and banana daiquiris and her beautiful, long legs brown on the beach in July and fresh chicken on the grill with Long Island local corn for dinner. He loved the outside of things—the tinkling of wine glasses at sunset and their cocktail parties with disco on the radio, crowds of bronzed, thin couples dancing on the deck. He loved the way his hair was soft and dark against his tan skin and the new shape his muscles were taking on—he loved the lightness of it all. He'd loved his work, too, then, the rush of secretaries around him adhering to his every wish; he loved to dictate letters and to research a case for court and to win that case. It was satisfying, winning like that, logical. He loved the judge and the celebratory lunch after wearing a good suit and eating a good steak and salad at P.J.'s, the slaps on the back from impressed partners when he walked into a party with her at his side, radiant and golden and so beautiful he sometimes had to watch her while she slept, amazed it was real, her beauty.

BUSINESS REPLY MAIL
FIRST CLASS MAIL   PERMIT NO. 17218-526   PITTSBURGH, PA

POSTAGE WILL BE PAID BY ADDRESSEE

CREATIVE NONFICTION
PO BOX 3000
DENVILLE NJ 07834-9259

NO POSTAGE
NECESSARY
IF MAILED
IN THE
UNITED STATES

BUSINESS REPLY MAIL
FIRST CLASS MAIL   PERMIT NO. 17218-526   PITTSBURGH, PA

POSTAGE WILL BE PAID BY ADDRESSEE

CREATIVE NONFICTION
PO BOX 3000
DENVILLE NJ 07834-9259

But she was strong, not fragile as she looked, and practical, and he loved, too, their talks in the car with the windows down on summer Sunday nights, the child asleep across their laps still sprinkled with sand from the beach and their skin hot from the day in the sun. She'd give him advice about a case or how to deal with his mother at Thanksgiving or what they should do with the kitchen, and they'd stop for ice-cream cones just before Exit 70, and the cones would drip down their shirts, cars speeding by and their little girl still sleeping soundly in the front seat, her face pressed so hard against the leather that it left a pattern on her cheek he could trace with his thumb as he carried her later into their building and to her bed as she never stirred. The girl he met by the lake in the Midwest one September afternoon was still always there, ready to laugh, to carry, to cook for 10 people he happened to meet on the train, to smile into the camera, and he didn't think he'd ever told her that.

What he hated were those looks she'd give him at dinner sometimes, her eyes silently begging for time with him alone. He craved action: 10 hours of a long day at the office and then a hot game of tennis, dinner afterward with six or seven people drinking and dancing. He craved the mad crush in the mornings on West End Avenue of well-dressed people rushing to work, hurrying to hail a cab, the exotic, expensive texture in his nostrils of perfume in the elevator at the U.N., the buzzing of cars on Madison Avenue as he gazed at windows filled with French antiques, silk scarves patterned with zebras and tropical fruits, long, white robes and hand-carved, walnut cigarette holders, richly colored oriental rugs and brave new abstract watercolors from the south of France, from Tahiti, from those places that sounded so wonderful he wanted to go just to say he'd been there. He'd get lost in those windows on Sunday afternoons, wandering in and out of bookshops and Bloomingdale's, stopping to pick up a bag of fresh apricots or a steaming rye bread from Zabar's. He would imagine her in the diamonds he saw in the windows as they left children with the nanny. He'd picture himself on the cover of Time, running for mayor. Whole afternoons passed this way. He liked to do it alone.

My hands trembling and cold, I hang up the phone after Layla's call. At 28 I am still floundering to escape the thickness of remembering that floods and captures me. I am my father; I am Layla; I am all the voices and wants and angers and stories and secrets. I keep rewinding the phone call, playing it over in my mind: Layla says to me again in her quiet way that her father died of AIDS. My breathing catches and twists. Her voice could make anyone love her. It is that gravelly, that soft, that full of princesses with long hair to climb up. It's been six years since we've spoken, and I don't know what to say. I finally tell her I have had dreams where Dad is dying alone, shivering in a surgical, metal-colored room, each beat of his heart the chiming of a bell.

Six years since I've heard her voice. I could almost kill something small, feel it crumble in my hands, when I think of how just before college she took the boy I thought was mine, the first I loved. Drunk in a cheap motel somewhere near Honfleur, France, she let him do things to her.

Here in Arizona I go back in my mind sometimes to those steepled evenings of snowy, violet twilight in New York when I was 13, as I'd climb the museum steps, waiting for her, waiting for my father to come home, waiting, freezing wind whipping a charcoal color around stark buildings, snow and rain slanting sideways. I'd imagine I was a girl in a book, a great dancer, a foreign spy, step after step.

I miss the moodiness of storms there, the way Layla and I stayed up so late some nights, talking and touching shoulders in constant rain, drifting off on each other to wake sleepily again, tangled, the endless drumming of rain pelting the windows.

Everyone's gay in my life, it seems. Layla and that boy both are now, and our fathers—hers and mine—and all that they know. I tried that, too, but it just didn't cut clean through me in the same way, that indigo slice that turns over inside the way a fish darts a perfect silver arc off the lake at dawn. The trees starting to turn color. That's what it feels like, a man's hands touching me softly that way, when it's real and we're there together.

Listening to her on the phone after six years is like breathing in sharp, salt air, like spinning around in circles until I'm dizzy and drunk. Her voice cuts through all the losses and years, brings back the hope for loving the way it should be, the way we prayed it would be as we sat on the pier looking out at New Jersey, the new morning always in the distance, no matter what.

I am 15 in the Hamptons with my dad, studying for a test, and he is scoping the beach of tanned, blond men in tight, black Speedos. We argue over the best-looking one. I insist that the Italian guy with glasses is my favorite, and he frowns and says, "Who raised *you*, anyway?" But we are also in the car on the way home, my head sleepily on his shoulder as he quizzes me on Latin vocabulary and worries that I will be tired in school tomorrow. "Remember," he says in his serious voice, "*Agricola* is a masculine word, though it's conjugated in the feminine." We are all of these things.

Eliot Sloan completed a master of fine arts degree in creative writing from the University of Arizona in 2001 and will complete a master of arts degree in English literature this summer from the Bread Loaf School of English. She has been published in the Washington Monthly, Vassar Review and Arizona Jewish newspaper. She also was awarded the English Poetry Award by the Bread Loaf School and the May Clayton Hayes Award for Creative Writing from the University of Arizona.

Aristotle's Ghost

Kurt Schwenk

I am white. I am male. The closest I come to prejudice every day is to suffer the baldness jokes of friends and comedians. I don't mind. Really. But I wonder—if most people were bald, would there be jokes about hairy scalps? Who is ridiculed and why? I watch a television documentary one night. It is the story of a group of physically disabled people attempting a difficult hike to the top of a mountain. Wheelchairs are muscled over boulders. One man pulls himself over logs and stones, powerful arms straining, immobile legs dragging behind. Another walks on his hands across a mountain stream. I am stunned by these scenes, awed by the spiritual and physical strength I see. I watch as an oncoming hiker passes by. "Why don't you get off the trail?" he sneers. I think I must have heard it wrong, but the narrator confirms it—not everyone is happy about the group being there. This offhand comment shocks and depresses me. How could someone feel anything but joy and admiration in the face of such determination and physical prowess? I have just witnessed one small, vile act of prejudice.

I am not naive. I know that prejudice is everywhere, all around us. It is as much a part of the human condition as language and upright stance. It issues from the human mixture, a noxious byproduct of diversity. Images of the Holocaust, ethnic cleansings, race riots are fresh in my mind. But like so much one learns or observes at a distance, these things are intellectualized. The small incident I have watched is so raw and unexpected it reaches from the screen and slaps me. I brood about it. There is no target for my outrage. The sneering tone of the man's voice—there was hate there, disgust, arrogance and superiority, all of it. What could provoke it? Hikers pass on a trail. They share the same enthusiasm. But one walks; the others do not. A small difference between them. A difference measured in chance.

Why do the differences among us lead to ridicule, to sneering, even to hate? Is prejudice inevitable? There seems to be a kind of terrible logic operating here, a hateful syllogism: People are different; differences create prejudice; people are prejudiced. As a scientist, an evolutionary biologist, I worry that it could be the way we are made, a hard-wired trap. At the same time, I am only too aware of how culture and the history of ideas shape our thoughts even before they are consciously manifested. Patterns of thought and therefore attitudes seem to develop in the mind along paths of least resistance. The paths become rutted with constant use and increasingly hard to escape. They may be more learned than evolved, and so I wonder about the history of ideas about diversity. Could the way we think about the diversity of life in the broadest sense provide clues to the nature of human prejudice? Is Aristotle to blame?

More than 300 years before the birth of Christ, Aristotle was busy establishing the roots of Western science. A keen observer of nature, he wrote voluminously about the animal life known to him. Like all biologists since, Aristotle needed a systematic way to arrange the creatures he described, a logical way to organize them for description and study. He recognized that certain groups of animals could be placed together on the basis of similarities in structure and that these were separated from other such groups by gaps or discontinuities in form or internal organization. To Aristotle the groups exhibited different levels of complexity that could be ordered from simplest to most complex. Aristotle thus organized all animal life into an ascending, linear sequence, or "scale of beings." Not surprisingly we humans were at the top of the heap (exalted by virtue of our "rational soul" and "high degree of life"). Diversity, Aristotle seemed to say, can be rank-ordered—and there's only room for one at the top.

The scale of beings, or *scala naturae* (ladder of nature), as it came to be called, became a mainstay of biological and religious thought. It permeated scientific thinking and our view of the world for more than 2,000 years after Aristotle's death. Christian theologians readily incorporated it into their doctrine, offering the harmony of nature as evidence of God's design. Species were viewed as fixed, each playing its essential role in the hierarchy. Indeed the very continuity of the chain of life was itself held as proof of divine perfection. Created in God's image and manifesting both the physical and the spiritual, human beings bridged the ethereal gap between animals and angels. German transcendentalists of the 19th century even invoked a parallel scale of beings in human development, seeing in the growth and transformation of embryos a sequential progression from "lower" to "higher" animal forms. Biologists of the time scrambled to describe the myriad new species then coming to light, working hard to fit them into the order of things, to place each one on the appropriate rung of the ladder.

The essential quality of the *scala naturae* was its equation of difference with rank, the conflation of diversity and sequence. Its consequence was vertical thinking—the notion that differences among types betrayed position in a vertical hierarchy. Different forms of life could be ordered, one above, one below, with all that this implies: lower-higher, imperfect-perfect, inferior-superior. As it was humans who created the order in the first place, it is hardly a surprise that they were placed at the top of this pecking order. From our 21st-century vantage point, we might further surmise that Aristotle and those who followed him did not have in mind just any humans for the coveted top position. The pinnacle was reserved for the leaders of the Western scientific and religious establishment—that is to say, white males like them.

Darwin, of course, should have ended it. Although not the first evolutionist, he was the first to propose a logical mechanism (natural selection) whereby one species could, over time, be transformed into another. He supported his theory with an overwhelming body of evidence. In one fell swoop, Darwin's 1859 "Origin of Species" dealt a decisive intellectual blow to vertical thinking. Implicit in his work was a new view of diversity—a richer, subtler, three-dimensional picture that emphasized historical equivalence, connection and kinship among all living forms rather than rank order. Instead of a straight line or an ascending series, Darwin's metaphor was a branching tree—the tree of life. In convincing the world of his views, Darwin confronted not only religious dogma but also the apparently innate resistance of people to truths of subtlety and complexity when a simpler preconception would seem to suffice. That Darwin won the battle but lost the war may be the point of this essay.

To understand the Darwinian view of diversity, we can turn to his metaphor of the tree. Imagine a fine, healthy specimen, dense with branches and twigs. At the point where the tree is widest, use virtual clippers to make an even cut all the way across so that everything above this point is removed, leaving a level plane. Lay a sheet of glass across the flat top of the truncated tree, and our model of diversity is complete. The glass plate is the present time, and the tree beneath the plate is the genealogical history of life on earth. At the base of the tree is a single trunk representing the origin of life more than three and a half billion years ago. Moving up from the base, branches diverge as ancestral species split into descendant daughter species, creating new, separately evolving lineages. Through geological time, countless branches split off, and new forms ceaselessly evolve. Tracing upward along any random path of connected branches, we discover that ultimately most branches end before reaching as high as the glass plate. These are the extinct lineages of life, a smattering known to us through their fossil remains. The extinct forms are legion, vastly outnumbering the few branches that make it all the way to the glass, the present time.

Scanning across the plate at the top of the tree, we see the yellow tips of each freshly shorn branch where it contacts the glass. These are the species of our present time, the lucky few to make it, the lineages that avoided extinction. They encompass the diversity of life on earth as we know it. Here is a parasitic worm, there a sponge. Farther along are frogs, and not too far from them, fishes, crocodiles and lizards. There are antelope, yeasts, bacteria, giant squids, oak trees, cormorants, algae, paramecia, locusts, moray eels, deer ticks and centipedes— diversity almost beyond imagining. Some of these life forms are simple, microscopic specks, hardly more than a strand of DNA surrounded by a membrane. Others are indescribably complex, vast conglomerations of specialized cells, pulsating organs, jointed legs, moving fluids and bulging brains packed with millions of sparking neurons. A few of them are human beings.

Now look again at the species disposed across the plane of glass. There is no vertical here. No higher, no lower, no rank order. There is no ladder. Only the horizontal now. Every form of life now extant has exactly the same amount of evolutionary history beneath it. Every species is equally evolved since the origin of life. Diversity is arrayed across a single plane of equivalence. From simple to complex, from *E. coli* to the leader of the Free World, each species—each individual—is at precisely the same level.

The tree shows more, however. It reveals the shared history of all life and the illusion of our separateness. For in the past, beneath the glass, the twigs of the present coalesce into common, ancestral stems, and these join still others farther back. Progressing downward, back through time, more and more branches merge until finally there is just the one trunk, symbol of that astonishing moment when inanimate became animate and the saga of genetic continuity began. Viewed from the present, the history of life is a story of confluence and connection, a fractal pattern of nested relationships. From this perspective we see that the question is not *if* we are related but only how closely.

Today, evolution is established fact—as well established as the rotation of the earth around the sun, the atomic nature of matter or the many other scientific certainties that can be proven, if not easily observed. Although technically still a "theory," natural selection has been demonstrated in nature and in the laboratory. All that remains is minor professional quibbling over mechanistic details and the relative importance of selection as the engine of evolutionary change in particular cases. In other words the Darwinian view of diversity has been fully vindicated. Aristotle's ladder has been replaced by the horizontal plane of evolutionary equivalence. Disparity, fixity of type and rank-order linearity are superceded by underlying similarity, historical confluence and the branching tree of life. Currently observed similarities and differences among species reflect only degrees of evolutionary relatedness, not absolutes—great similarity implies a relatively recent divergence from a common ancestral form, with increasing difference roughly proportional to the time since a historical, genealogical split between lineages. Thus it is that our kinship to a chimpanzee is readily apparent, separated as we are by only a few million years (a geological instant), but our connection to the oyster slurped at dinner or the grass trod underfoot is hidden to the casual eye by the eons passed since our genetic lines shook hands and parted ways.

The Darwinian view of diversity applies equally to humans and other species. As for all life existing in the present, human differences reflect equivalences, not positions in a hierarchy. Prejudice is not possible in a society enlightened by Darwinian thinking because there is no basis for rank-ordering, no way to place one type—one race, one ethnicity, one religion, one culture, one sex—above another. Prejudice is spawned by vertical thinking, the scientifically vitiated practice of turning diversity on end, rending the connections among us, and stacking the differences in arbitrary order, only one at the top. What could be more unnatural, more irrational or more hateful? What could be more common?

OK, perhaps I am naive, after all. Who ever said prejudice is rational? But I can't help wondering. I'm a scientist, after all, a professional rationalist. I naturally seek patterns and the causal processes underlying them. Prejudice follows a well-worn and unusually persistent path in the history of scientific thought on diversity. Vertical, linear thinking has the advantage of more than 2,000 years over the principles of Darwinism. Perhaps its expression in modern human behavior reflects nothing more than the disjunction between scientific and everyday thinking, the typical lag between the origin of new knowledge and its assimilation into the general population. This implies that time and education are the remedies to the scourge of prejudice. In my optimistic periods, I almost believe this.

Optimists can find succor in evolutionary theory. Everything we know says that diversity in humans, as in other species, is good. It is the best possible hedge against extinction. From diversity emerges the highly desirable trait of "evolvability"—literally, the ability to evolve, to adapt to new conditions. If life is a game, there is only one measure of success: persistence. Losers go extinct. Those species at risk of extinction are usually those that are least diverse. Genetic and behavioral mechanisms exist in most species, including humans, to promote diversity. The evolution of sex itself is likely to have persisted in the face of severe competition from rapidly reproducing asexual forms, by virtue of the boost it gives to the creation of diversity and therefore evolvability. Genetically homogenized human populations are more likely to express undesirable recessive traits and genetic diseases. "Outcrossing" among divergent populations creates healthier offspring. Humans, for example, usually select mates that differ immunologically, an unconscious preference mediated by smell that leads to healthier, more disease-resistant children. Our experience with commercially bred agricultural monocultures teaches us the extreme danger of uniformity—whole crops are wiped out by single pathogens because nowhere in the population are resistant individuals to be found. The lack of diversity can be fatal. Why would a human monoculture fare any better?

Everything points to one thing—diversity is good for us, both in the short term and in the long term. It makes us healthier, stronger and more likely to survive as individuals and as a species. Without it we would go extinct in short order. Even as the bigots among us work outwardly to expunge diversity, to move us toward monoculture, they are betrayed by the inner workings of their own bodies, belied by physiology, sexual desire and the unconscious mind—like it or not, bigots do their small part for diversity. Human diversity is not just an accident of geography; it is an evolved strategy for survival. To succumb to prejudice, to idealize the monoculture, is to work against one's own best interests.

We are left with a paradox. Diversity is good for us, but it leads to prejudice, which works against it. The rational study of diversity leads to a conception of human differences distributed across a horizontal plane of equivalence and connected by common descent, but our irrational reaction to these differences is to isolate them in denial of our connection and to rank them one above the other according to some arbitrary and self-serving scheme. The *scala naturae* and vertical thinking were supplanted by Darwinism more than a century ago, but the ghost of Aristotle still haunts us.

It is possible that prejudice will dissipate before an advancing front of education and enlightenment, but I fear something more insidious than ignorance. We need only look around us to see that education is no certain cure. If it were, evolutionary biologists would be the least prejudiced among us, and sadly, this is not true (how many geneticists supported eugenics programs?). The truth is that vertical thinking may be less about history and education than it is about the workings of the human mind. We may all be infected to some extent. It is difficult, maybe impossible, to escape. Even our language betrays us. Many biologists, who should know better, still refer to "lower" and "higher" animals, implying both sequence and status where there is none. How many of us believe that humans evolved from monkeys? If you so believe, you have done it, however unwittingly—you have twisted the horizontal plane of equivalence to a vertical sequence. Monkeys did not beget humans. They are not imperfect versions of us, a step along the way to humanity. There is no straight line connecting us. Rather, monkey and human lineages sprang from a common ancestor, a creature that was neither monkey nor human. The line connecting us is a V, each of us sharing equal status at the top. Our extinct common ancestor lies at the conjoined base of our lineages, buried in the past, a single point of departure for our now-separate lineages. Along the way our own lineage gave off its own branches—gibbon, orangutan, gorilla and chimpanzee. These are not our ancestors; they are our brothers, our sisters, our cousins, our evolutionary equals.

I lecture about these principles to my students, and for a while, they seem to grasp them, to leave the straight lines and the *scala naturae* behind. But there are signs that soon even they will slip back into vertical thinking, all sense of common ancestry and equal evolutionary status gone. They will revert to the notion that salamanders evolved from fish, that lizards evolved from salamanders and that mammals evolved from lizards. And, yes, that humans evolved from monkeys. The march from low to high, from slimy to hairy, from sprawled to upright seems so inevitable and direct, so very seductive. Vertical thinking is the path of least resistance, and therein lies the rub.

My suspicion is that as humans we share an innate tendency to prefer simple over complex explanations for the patterns we confront. Perhaps it is an act of self-defense in the face of the chaos that would otherwise overwhelm us. Indeed scientists themselves are fond of simple explanations, perhaps overly fond, preferring them to arguments of greater complexity. Direct or straightforward solutions to difficult problems are often described as *elegant*, an overworked word meaning, in scientific parlance, "beautifully simple." To have the word *elegant* attached to one's work is to be paid a great compliment. Such attitudes betray a seemingly reasonable yet unsubstantiated faith in Occam's razor, the principle stating that no more assumptions should be made in explaining a thing than are necessary. It is applied as a general rule in most sciences and is even used as the basis for choice among competing theories—all else being equal, the simplest explanation is accepted as most likely to be true. In evolutionary biology Occam's razor is codified in the "rule of parsimony," which asserts that simple evolutionary transitions, or transformations involving the fewest steps, are to be preferred over less direct or longer pathways. The problem is that there is little evidence to support such choices.

Indeed there are many examples to the contrary. More to the point is the indication that even the professionals charged with developing formal explanations for natural phenomena are seduced by simplicity.

Simple explanations resonate. They reassure and comfort us. They are more easily grasped and held in the mind, retained long after more complex chains of argument are lost to memory. They are preferred by a media establishment intent on reducing complex phenomena to simple, digestible bits that won't challenge consumers or encroach upon the next commercial. I feel helpless in the face of this onslaught. Everything I learn reveals a world of stunning complexity. The dogs of chaos are barking at my heels, and I think perhaps it's just me—I've come up against my intellectual limits, my capacity to understand, and it is my own inadequacy I fear. But this much I know: Sometimes the most important truths are subtle and complex. They are difficult to understand, hard to explain, harder to remember. They are anything but elegant.

I am left with the echo of that sneering voice in my mind: "Why don't you get off the trail?" I feel little better now, but at least I see the hateful remark for what it was—a violent intrusion of vertical thinking into a horizontal world. My exercise in rationalism has shown me that this knee-jerk tendency to sort fellow human beings along an ascending scale of value is at least concordant with ancient scientific and religious practice. There is the possibility of historical inertia acting here. But the chain of causality is by no means certain, for there is also the intimation that vertical thinking reflects little more than our own cognitive limitations, with prejudice an unfortunate sequela. Modern prejudice may indeed have its roots in ancient views of diversity, but I fear that both find common cause in the dark workings of the human mind—one thing, at least, we all share.

Kurt Schwenk *is an evolutionary biologist and professor of ecology and evolutionary biology at the University of Connecticut. He has a bachelor's in biology from Oberlin College and a doctorate in zoology from the University of California, Berkeley. He has served as a scientific consultant for television and published more than 40 scientific papers, as well as several popular essays in Science Magazine, Natural History Magazine and the New York Times Book Review. Schwenk resides in Storrs, Conn.*

Going Native

Francine Prose

*S*everal years ago at an elementary-school Christmas play in upstate New York, I sat behind three fourth-graders from the most remote and poorest section of the rural school district. In all likelihood the boys had never seen an actual African-American person except on television and on rare trips to Kingston, 40 miles away. Nonetheless they wore their version of authentic gangsta attire: huge windpants, baggy sweatshirts, baseball caps turned backward. During one confusing scene—something about Santa looking for his elves—one of the boys turned to his friends and said, "Yo, man, whassup? What that mothafucka be saying?"

For these little boys, the identification with inner-city kids ran deeper than a taste for rap music and the urge to make a fashion statement. In their secret hearts, they were the black kids who—had they actually met them—would have ignited their prejudices and their secret fear of flesh-and-blood (as opposed to fantasy) African-Americans. For these isolated white kids, victims of a rural poverty more hidden and less readily acknowledged than its urban counterpart, the African-American musicians they saw on MTV were saying something that they felt but could not express for themselves—voicing their alienation, their disenfranchisement, their sense of being exiled to the fringes of a society that would prefer they didn't exist. Likewise the appealing young men and women in Alan Parker's film "The Commitments"—poor Northern Irish kids without a lot of career prospects who form a soul band specializing in the greatest hits of Aretha Franklin and Otis Redding—are drawn to the music for reasons that go beyond the music, and the gifted young performers joke about their identification with the poverty, alienation and disenfranchisement of African-Americans.

Something of this sort—but stranger and more complex—is currently going on among the white working class and rural poor who attend regional powwows and decorate their homes with images representing a sort of airbrushed, mythical, Disneyfied version of the Native-American experience. Every summer I visit the same flea market in central Tennessee, and each year there are more stands selling clocks, rugs, paintings and countless household items depicting beautiful Indian maidens and muscular braves in buckskins and feathered headdresses.

Of course cartoonish images of Native Americans have long adorned cultural artifacts ranging from heroic, commemorative historical paintings to the hoods of automobiles to the logos of football teams. But what seems to have changed is that the people most drawn to these symbols have increasingly convinced themselves that they *are* Native Americans, or close to it. With just a little cultural fantasizing, whites—conveniently ignoring the fact that the land their flea market stands on originally belonged to Native Americans—can see themselves as the authentic, self-sufficient, proud people, close to the land and valiantly defending traditional ways against the incursions of the Other: rich, white, urban, or alternately, immigrant or African-American.

So for the past several years, a small community in New York's Hudson Valley has been severely divided and damaged by a conflict over whether to retire the Indian that serves as the local high school's logo. Much of the pressure to get rid of the hideous, racist cartoon has come from the more politically liberal elements of the Onteora school district, which includes families who have moved up from Manhattan and the suburbs, as well as the areas' few minority and immigrant families. But conservatives—more likely to be older retirees and working people, economically embattled and fearing political disenfranchisement—have fought bitterly to retain the image, which on some level they sincerely believe to be an image of themselves. If the symbol disappears, they feel that a link to their past will be taken away. So what if it's not *their* past, exactly? The logo makes them feel part of a larger community with a braver history than their own; they're the Iroquois nation, just as their kids imagine themselves as the gangstas in the Wu-Tang clan.

"Going native" embraces a myth of what a culture represents and makes it one's own myth—a handy process when at the moment there isn't a viable myth to explain our experience or to make us feel better about ourselves. If for example the American dream no longer describes the arc of our personal history or seems like a possible goal, we must seek another fantasy—an altered notion of who we are or who we might become. The desire or the need to go native reminds us of how much about our most basic identity is subject to a certain slippage—particularly in certain individuals who for personal reasons require the equivalent of cosmetic psychic surgery. They need not only to surround themselves with the Other; they need to become the Other.

The trouble arises, of course, when the person or people who have gone native lose sight of the actual lives of the actual group they imagine they are. They fail to acquire any special sympathy for the people with whose culture they identify (why do I doubt that the kids at my school's Christmas play are going to grow up to be campaigners for civil rights?) and may even resent the group for actually existing and thus spoiling the fantasy of the gone-native. It's one thing to have a Big Chief air freshener hanging from your dashboard; it's quite another to believe that the Native Americans are entitled to all the profits from the bingo casino in your county.

For many reasons, going native is frequently unattractive, and our distaste often expresses itself in ways that combine the visceral and the aesthetic. Our feelings about the Hare Krishna movement are not unaffected by the fact that pink and orange are unflattering colors for white kids so wan and pale they look nearly transparent. Our image of the gone-native evokes, more often than not, the tubby, middle-aged white guy in a sarong in a thatched hut, snacking on some local delicacy cooked by his beautiful child bride.

Part of our unease stems from the fact that going native has traditionally involved a certain amount of sexual colonialism and imperialist exploitation. It is hard not to feel protective of the very young men whose photos turn up (with captions like "My loyal guide, Fariq") in the biographies and travel journals of such legendary voyagers as Wilfred Thesiger and T.E. Lawrence, in anthropological studies and in accounts of American expatriate artists—for example, in the social circle surrounding the Beats and Paul Bowles in North Africa. In the popular imagination, going native often invokes an element of hands-on, anthropological research. This response is partly what Conrad is trading on in "Heart of Darkness": the notion of the white man who has left the clean light of day to tunnel deep into the jungly nether regions of sex, death and God knows what else.

Perhaps the most famous cultural figure to have gone native is Paul Gauguin—a beloved figure almost as adored as Van Gogh, or maybe more so. In our own mythology, he's the big, life-loving, Anthony Quinn character, leaving his chilly, French middle-class life, lighting out for Paradise, from where he dispatches idyllic telegraphs from a world of luminous color, populated by graceful, mysterious, beautiful women perfectly in tune with their surroundings.

His journal, "Noa Noa," tells a somewhat different story. Arriving in Papeete on an "artistic mission" which the local governor assumed to be espionage, Gauguin was soon dissatisfied with the port city—so full of Europeans!—and resolved to go inland. His Papeete *vahini*, Titi, had a lot to recommend her: "The amorous passion of a Maori courtesan is something quite different from the passivity of a Parisian cocotte—something very different! There is fire in her blood, which calls forth love as its essential nourishment; which exhales it like fatal perfume." But she also had an insurmountable flaw, and soon enough he left her because her ancestry, he felt, would prevent her from initiating him in the cultural or sexual mysteries which he fantasized experiencing with a lover of purer extraction: "It was her half-white blood...I felt that she could not teach me any of the things I wished to know, that she had nothing to give of that special happiness which I sought."

After Gauguin had been in his inland village long enough to get lonely, his neighbors brought him a "large child" on whom "two swelling buds rose on the breasts." Worried at first that the girl had been forced into marriage by her mother, the artist was reassured "when I saw in the face of the young girl, in her gestures and attitude the distinct signs of independence and pride which are characteristic of her race." Despite age, cultural and language differences, the artist and his wife, Tehura, fell deeply in love, and she was the last thing he saw as he sailed back to France for a two-year stay, after which he returned to Tahiti, where he would die in 1903. "She had wept through many nights. Now she sat worn-out and sad, but calm, on a stone with her legs hanging down and her strong, lithe feet touching the soiled water... The flower which she had put behind the ear in the morning had fallen wilted upon her knee."

Such accounts only reinforce our discomfort with the solipsistic romanticization, the racism and exploitation involved in going native, with the narcissistic projection, the frequent inability to see the actual human beings behind (and possibly contradicting) the myth. How, for example, did Gauguin ascertain that his child bride had decided to marry him of her own free will when, at least at the beginning, neither spoke the other's language? But are there cases which seem to us non-exploitative, in which we intuit that something not merely beneficial but essential transpires for the individual and for the community in which an old identity is traded for a new one?

Since there are, as we now know, transsexuals—men and women who grow up knowing instinctively and beyond persuasion that they have been doomed to inhabit a body with a different gender from their brain and heart—surely there must be transculturals—people who have been born in the wrong society and for whom going native represents the equivalent of a surgical correction.

For a while I believed that about myself. From 1969 to 1970, I spent almost a year in India, from which I returned convinced that I should have been born there. Everything about Indian society—the bad as well as the good—seemed preferable and more sensible than the one I had left, in Cambridge, Mass. The colors were brighter, the people handsomer, the culture richer. I was happier there than I'd ever been—and certainly happier than I'd been in Cambridge in graduate school, living with the college boyfriend I'd married during my senior year at Radcliffe. I was miserable, and after months spent attending one class every morning and watching TV for the remaining hours, I began to think that I was losing my mind. Eventually I asked my husband—a graduate student in math—where he could take his fellowship and still get academic credit. I skimmed the list he brought home and realized that the Tata Institute of Fundamental Research in Colaba, Bombay, was as far as I could possibly get from Harvard Square.

Ten months later we landed in India. I didn't sleep for three nights. In the dark when I closed my eyes, my mind replayed choppy silent films from the day: naked *sadhus* with tridents, covered with ash and feathers; bony cows, like tent poles with skin, freely grazing the vegetable stalls; men in white holding hands, drifting over the dusty maidan; the dust that coated everything; the homeless families living on the sidewalks, at the station, sleeping on string cots, cooking on camp stoves.

Much of what I saw terrified me, yet I was intensely happy, perhaps because my fear was the closest thing I'd felt in months to a genuine emotion, but also because I'd already fallen in love with the excess, the overabundance: too many people, too much to see, too much noise, too many bright colors. It seemed less like overload than replenishment after the sensory-deprivation tank in which I'd been living.

This new world around me was dizzying and chaotic. And I recovered my mental health within a matter of days. I knew what pleased me (the smell of *bidi* cigarettes, of burning cowshit, of curry, the children's kohl-rimmed eyes, the brilliant saris and bangles, the little pyramids of spices and lapidary dyes in the market) and what saddened and enraged me (the cruelty of the caste system, the bleating of the lepers, the glassy stare of the beggar-women's babies, the families living in drainage culverts).

I was too ironic, too much of a snob to wear a sari, which makes European women look so awkward and awful. But I did pick up a trace of an Indian accent and the ability to shake my head *no* to mean *yes*, a language of intonation and gesture that made it easier to communicate with my neighbors in Bombay. I wore embroidered Indian shirts and let the sun darken my face until I could pass for Indian, especially among people who didn't know any better. Traveling back to the United States, I stopped in London and was secretly pleased (when, for example, my unfamiliarity with the British monetary system inspired some racist mumbling from a woman in a tobacco shop) to be taken for a different sort of foreigner than I actually was.

When I returned to America, I imagined that I would stay just long enough to get my life in order, long enough to arrange for a speedy turnaround, after which I would go back to my real country —India. But of course things didn't work out that way. Life, as they say, intervened. Seven years passed before I returned, as a tourist— and knew that was what I was.

In my case going native represented the equivalent of a reversible operation. Some of the effects on me were permanent. I had learned the obvious lesson that things were different elsewhere, that disparate cultures could view the world in entirely dissimilar ways. And I like to think that, for me, the experience helped to enlarge the tiny little prison of the self to which we are mostly confined.

But there are instances of going native that are more final, life-changing and irreversible, capable of curing a sense of dislocation, the unhappy conviction of having been born in the wrong place. Surely for some individuals, going native constructs or reconstructs the person who should have been born in the adopted home.

Probably the most striking example is that of Lafcadio Hearn. Born in 1850 in Greece to a local woman and an Irish Protestant surgeon in the British army, Hearn was brought as a child to Dublin, where he was abandoned by his parents and raised by a great-aunt. His physical appearance—he was extremely short and nearly blind from a childhood accident—contributed to his sense of alienation, homelessness and exile. After sojourns in Ohio and New Orleans, where he worked as a reporter, and an early marriage to a half-black woman named Alethea Foley, Hearn left for Japan in 1890. There he found a succession of jobs as an English instructor, a journalist, a translator and finally as a teacher at Tokyo and Waseda universities.

Soon after arriving in Japan, he wrote to a friend, "I only wish I could be reincarnated in some little Japanese baby, so that I could see and feel the world as beautifully as a Japanese brain does." And from the beginning, he felt that he had come home, that (after a lifetime of believing that he was doomed to peripatetic solitude) he finally comprehended and was capable of being accepted by the world around him. He described a sort of existential déjà vu—a sense of being surrounded by "strange Gods. I seem to have known and loved them before somewhere."

Not long after his arrival, Hearn entered into an arranged marriage with a Japanese woman, with whom he had four children. He became a Japanese citizen and assumed a Japanese name. He took financial responsibility for his wife's extended family and evolved into a beloved and revered patriarch—a position in society which could hardly have been more different from his lonely, marginal existence in England and the United States.

In Japan Hearn discovered not only his subject (his best books are redactions of Japanese folk tales) but also a literary aesthetic; he abandoned his formerly elaborate prose style and pursued "perfect simplicity." His most basic values shifted to reflect those of his adopted culture: "I have nine lives depending on my work—wife,

wife's mother, wife's father, wife's adopted mother, wife's father's father, and then servants, and a Buddhist student…You can't let a little world grow up around you, to depend on you, and then break it all up—not if you are a respectable person. And I indulge in the luxury of 'filial piety'—a virtue of which the good and evil results are known only to us Orientals." He looked back with wonder and more than a little horror on his "old self as of something which ought not to have been allowed to exist on the face of the earth— and yet, in my present self, I sometimes feel ghostly reminders that the old self was very real indeed." And he succumbed—with deep pleasure and gratitude—to the rewards and domestic satisfactions of his life as a Japanese husband and father: "I should find living away from all Europeans rather hard, if it were not for the little world I have made around me…at home I enter into my little smiling world of old ways and thoughts and courtesies…It has become Me."

So what are we to make of this case in which going native is not a process of self-obliteration but of self-discovery, not a matter of colonialism and sexual or cultural exploitation but of genuine appreciation of—and contribution to—a society that proves in every way more congenial than the world that has been left behind? First it is a salutary reminder that our responses to the questions of assimilation and diversity (how much we should contribute to and take away from the melting pot) are as various, unpredictable and endlessly mysterious as every other aspect of human behavior. And finally it is a warning against easy judgments and facile formulations on the subject of cultural politics, and about the ways each of us stitches together an identity from the scraps we are able to collect from the world just outside—and far beyond—our doorstep.

Francine Prose's highly acclaimed works of fiction include "Blue Angel," "Bigfoot Dreams," "Household Saints," "Hunters and Gatherers," "Primitive People" and "Guided Tours of Hell: Novellas." Her work has appeared in The New Yorker, Atlantic Monthly, GQ and Paris Review. She is a contributing editor at Harper's Magazine and writes about art for the Wall Street Journal. Prose's numerous grants and awards include a Guggenheim and a Fulbright, and she is Director's Fellow at the Center for Scholars and Writers at the New York Public Library. She has taught at Iowa Writers' Workshop, Sewanee Writers' Conference and Johns Hopkins University. She lives in New York City.

Looking at Emmett Till

John Edgar Wideman

—for Qasima

A nightmare of being chased has plagued my sleep since I was a boy. The monster pursuing me assumes many shapes, but its face is too terrifying for the dream to reveal. Even now I sometimes startle myself awake, screaming, the dream's power undiminished by time, the changing circumstances of my waking life.

I've come to believe the face in the dream I can't bear to look upon is Emmett Till's. Emmett Till's face, crushed, chewed, mutilated, his gray face swollen, water dripping from holes punched in his skull. Warm, gray water on that August day in 1955 when they dragged his corpse from the Tallahatchie River. Emmett Till and I both 14 the summer they murdered him. The nightmare an old acquaintance by then, as old as anything I can remember about myself.

Yet the fact that the nightmare predates by many years the afternoon in Pittsburgh I came across Emmett Till's photograph in Jet magazine seems to matter not at all. The chilling dream resides in a space years can't measure, the boundless sea of Great Time, nonlinear, ever abiding, enfolding past, present and future.

I certainly hadn't been searching for Emmett Till's picture in Jet. It found me. A blurred, grayish something resembling an aerial snapshot of a landscape cratered by bombs or ravaged by natural disaster. As soon as I realized the thing in the photo was a dead black boy's face, I jerked my eyes away. But not quickly enough.

I attempted to read Jet's story about the murder without getting snagged again by the picture. Refusing to look, lacking the power to look at Emmett Till's face, shames me to this day. Dangerous and cowardly not to look. Turning away from his eyeless stare, I blinded

49

myself. Denied myself denying him. He'd been 14, like me. How could I be alive and Emmett Till dead? Who had killed him? Why? Would I recognize him if I dared look? Could my own features be horribly altered like his? I needed answers, needed to confront what frightened me in the murdered black boy's face. But Emmett Till just too dead, too gruesomely, absolutely dead to behold.

Years afterward during college I'd recall how it felt to discover Emmett Till's picture when one of my summer jobs involved delivering towels and sheets to the city morgue, and the booze-breathed old coroner who got his kicks freaking out rookies lifted a kettle's lid to prove, yes, indeed, there was a human skull inside from which he was attempting to boil the last shreds of meat.

Now when I freeze-frame a close-up shot of Emmett Till's shattered face on my VCR, am I looking? The image on the screen still denies its flesh-and-blood origins. It's a smashed, road-killed thing, not a boy's face. I'm reminded of the so-called "nail fetishes," West African wood sculptures, part mask, part free-standing head, that began appearing when slaving ships crisscrossed the Atlantic. Gouged, scarred, studded with nails, glass, cartridge shells, stones, drools of raffia, hunks of fur and bone, these horrific creatures police the boundary between human and spirit worlds. Designed to terrify and humble, they embody evil's power to transcend mere human conceptions of its force, reveal the chaos always lurking within the ordinary, remind us the gods amuse themselves by snatching away our certainties.

Whether you resided in an African-American community like Homewood, where I spent half my early years, or in white areas like Shadyside, with a few houses on a couple of streets for black people—my turf when we didn't live in my grandparents' house in Homewood—everybody colored knew what was in *Jet* magazine. *Jet*'s articles as much a part of our barbershop, poolroom, ball field, corner, before-and after-church talk as the *Courier*, Pittsburgh's once-a-week newspaper, aka the Black Dispatch. Everybody aware of *Jet* and the *Courier* even though not everybody approved or identified to the same degree with these publications, whose existence was rooted in an unblinking acknowledgment of the reality of racial segregation, a reality their contents celebrated as much as protested.

Jet would arrive at our house on Copeland Street, Shadyside, in batches, irregularly, when Aunt Catherine, who lived down the block and never missed an issue, finished with them and got around to dropping some off. Aunt Catherine was my father's sister, and they were Harry Wideman's kids and inherited his deep-brown, South Carolina skin, while my mother's side of the family was light, bright and almost white, like my other grandfather, Daddyjohn French, from Culpepper, Va.

Skin color in my family, besides being tattletale proof segregation didn't always work, was a pretty good predictor of a person's attitude toward Jet magazine. My mother wouldn't or couldn't buy Jet. I've never asked her which. In pale Shadyside, Jet wasn't on sale. You'd have to go a good distance to find it, and with neither car nor driver's license and five kids to care for 24/7, my mother seldom ranged very far from home. Tight as money was then, I'm sure a luxury like subscribing to Jet never entered her mind. If by some miracle spare change became available and Brackman's Pharmacy on Walnut Street had begun stocking Jet, my mother would have been too self-conscious to purchase a magazine about colored people from old, icy, frecklefingered Brackman.

Although apartheid stipulates black and white as absolutely separate categories, people construct day by day through the choices they make and allow to be made for them what constitutes blackness and whiteness, what race means, and Mr. Brackman presided over one of the whitest businesses on Walnut Street. Clearly he didn't want folks like us in his drugstore. His chilliness, disdain and begrudging service a nasty medicine you had to swallow while he doled out your prescriptions. White kids permitted to sit on the floor in a corner and browse through the comic-book bin, but he hurried me along if he thought I attempted to read before I bought. (I knew he believed I'd steal his comics if he turned his back, so in spite of his eagle eye, I did, with sweet, sweet satisfaction every chance I got, throwing them in a garbage can before I got home to avoid that other eagle eye, my mom's.)

Though copies reached us by a circuitous and untimely route, my mother counted on Jet. Read it and giggled over its silliness, fussed at its shamelessness, envied and scoffed at the airs of the "sididdy folks" who paraded through it weekly. In my grandparents' house in Homewood, when my mom got down with her sisters, Geraldine and Martha, I'd eavesdrop while they riffed on Jet's contents, fascinated by how they mixed Homewood people and gossip into Jet's features, improvising new stories, raps and sermons I'd never imagined when I'd read it alone.

By the time an issue of Jet reached me, after it had passed through the hands of Aunt Catherine, Uncle Horton, my mother, my father when he was around, the pages were curled, ink-smeared, soft and comfortable as Daddyjohn French's tobacco-ripe flannel shirts. I could fan the pages, and the widest gaps opened automatically at the best stories.

With its spatters, spots, rings from the bottom of a coffee cup, smudges of chocolate candy or lipstick, pages with turned-down corners, pages ripped out, torn covers, Jet was an image of the black world as I understood it then: secondhand, beat-up, second-rate. Briar patch and rebuke.

But also often truer and better than the other world around me. Much better. Jet, with its incriminating, renegade, embarrassing, topsy-turvy, loud, proud focus on colored doings and faces expanded my sense of possibility. Compared to other magazines of the '50s— Life, Look, House & Garden, Redbook—Jet was like WAMO, the radio station that blasted rhythm-and-blues and gospel, an escape from the droning mediocrity of "Your Hit Parade," a plunge into versions of my life unavailable elsewhere on the dial, grabbing me, shaking me up, reminding me life could move to a dance beat.

In 1955, the year Emmett Till was murdered, I, like him, had just graduated from junior high. I'm trying to remember if I, like him, carried pictures of white girls in my wallet. Can't recall whether I owned a wallet in 1955. Certainly it wouldn't have been a necessity since the little bits of cash I managed to get hold of passed rapidly through my hands. "Money burns a hole in your pocket, boy," my mom said. Wanting to feel grown up, manly, I probably stuffed some sort of hand-me-down billfold in my hip pocket, and carrying around a white girl's picture in it would have been ocular proof of sexual prowess, proof the color of my skin didn't scare white chicks away or scare me away from them. A sign of power. Proof I could handle that other world, master its opportunities and dangers. Since actual romances across the color line tended to be rare and clandestine then, a photo served as evidence of things unseen. A ticket to status in my tiny clan of Shadyside brown boys, a trophy copped in another country I could flaunt in black Homewood. So I may have owned a wallet with pictures of white girlfriends/classmates in it, and if I'd traveled to Promised Land, S.C., with my grandfather Harry Wideman one of those summers he offered to take me down home where he'd been born and raised, who knows? Since I was a bit of a smart aleck, like Emmett Till, I might have flashed my snapshots. I liked to brag. Take on dares like him. *Okay. Okay, Emmett Till. You so bad. You talking 'bout all those white gals you got up in Chicago. Bet you won't say boo to that white lady in the store.*

Two years before Emmett Till was beaten and murdered, when both Emmett Till and I were 12, a stroke killed my mother's father, John French. I lapsed into a kind of semi-coma, feverish, silent, sleeping away whole days, a little death to cope with losing my grandfather, my family believed. Grieving for Daddyjohn was only part of the reason I retreated into myself. Yes, I missed him. Everybody was right about that, but I couldn't confide to anyone that the instant he died, there was no room for him in my heart. Once death closed his eyes, I wanted him gone, utterly, absolutely gone. I erected a shell to keep him out, to protect myself from the touch of his ghostly hands, the smells and sounds of him still lurking in the rooms of the Homewood house where we'd lived for a year with my mother's parents and her sisters after my father left our house on Copeland Street.

Losing my grandfather stunned me. He'd been my best friend. I couldn't understand how he'd changed from Daddyjohn to some invisible, frightening presence I had no name for. He'd stopped moving, speaking, breathing. For two interminable days, his body lay inside a coffin on a spindly-legged, metal stand beside the piano in the living room, the dark, polished wood of one oblong box echoing the other. Until we had to sell the piano a few years later, I couldn't enter the room or touch the piano unless someone else was with me. Sitting on the spinning stool, banging away for hours on the keys had been one of my favorite solitary pastimes, as unthinkable suddenly as romping with my dead grandfather, chanting the nonsense rimes he'd taught me—"Froggy went a-courting, and he did ride/Uh-huh, uh-huh."

Stunned by how empty, how threatening the spaces of my grand-father's house had become, I fought during the daylight hours to keep him away, hid under the covers of my bed at night. Stunned by guilt. By my betrayal of him, my inability to remember, to honor the love that had bound us. Love suddenly changed to fear of everything about him. Fear that love might license him to trespass from the grave.

I'd never understood the dead. Shied away from talk of death, thoughts of the dead. The transformation of my grandfather the instant he became one of the dead confirmed my dread. If I couldn't trust Daddyjohn, what horrors would the rest of the dead inflict upon me? Given the nightmare's witness, am I still running, still afraid?

Emmett Till's murder was an attempt to slay an entire generation. Push us backward to the bad old days when our lives seemed not to belong to us. When white power and racism seemed unchallengeable forces of nature, when inferiority and subserviency appeared to be our birthright, when black lives seemed cheap and expendable, when the grossest insults to pride and person, up to and including murder, had to be endured. No redress, no retaliation, no justice expected. Emmett Till's dead body, like the body of James Byrd just yesterday in Texas, reminded us that the bad old days are never farther away than the thickness of skin, skin some people still claim the prerogative to burn or cut or shoot full of holes if it's dark skin. It's no accident that Emmett Till's dead face appears inhuman. The point of inflicting the agony of his last moments, killing and mutilating him, is to prove he's not human.

And it almost works. Comes close to working every time. Demon-ized by hot-blooded or cold-blooded statistics of crime, addiction, disease, cartooned, minstrelized, criminalized, eroticized, commodi-fied in stereotypical representations, the black body kidnapped and displayed by the media loses all vestiges of humanity. We are set back on our collective heels by the overwhelming evidence, the constant warning that beneath black skin something *other*, something brutal lurks. A so-called "lost generation" of young black men dying in the streets today points backward, the way Emmett Till's rotting corpse points backward, history and prophecy at once: This is the way things have always been, will always be, the way they're supposed to be.

The circle of racism, its perverse logic remain unbroken. Boys like Emmett Till are born violating the rules, aren't they? Therefore they forfeit any rights law-abiding citizens are bound to respect. The bad places—ghettos, prisons, morgue slabs—where most of them wind up confirm the badness of the boys. Besides, does it hurt any less if the mugger's a product of nurture, not nature? Keeping him off your streets, confining him in a world apart is what matters, isn't it?

But what if the disproportionate numbers of African-American males in prison or caught in the net of economic marginality are not a consequence of inborn, black deviancy? What if incarceration and poverty are latter-day, final solutions of the problem of slavery? What if the dismal lives of so many young black people indicate an intentional, systematic closing off of access to the mainstream, justified by a mythology of race that the closing off simultaneously engenders and preserves?

Nearly 500 years ago, European ships began transporting captive Africans to the New World. Economic exploitation of the recently "discovered" Americas provided impetus for this slave trade. Buying and selling African bodies, treating them as property, commodities, livestock produced enormous profit and imprinted a model for ignoring the moral and ethical implications of financially successful global commerce we continue to apply today. The traffic in human bodies was also fueled by a dream, a Utopian dream of escape from the poverty, disease, class and religious warfare of Europe, a dream of transforming through European enterprise and African slave labor the wilderness across the sea into a garden of wealth and prosperity, with the European colonist cast as the New Adam exercising divinely sanctioned dominion over all he surveyed.

Racism and genocide were the underside of this Edenic dream, persist today in the determined unwillingness of the heirs of the dream to surrender advantages gained when owning slaves was legal.

During its heyday slavery's enormous profit and enormous evil sparked continuous debate. Could a true Christian own slaves? Do Africans possess souls? Because it licensed and naturalized the subjugation of "inferior" Africans by "superior" Europeans, the invention of the concept of "race"—dividing humankind into a hierarchy of groups, each possessing distinct, unchangeable traits that define the groups as eternally separate and unequal—was crucial to the slaveholder's temporary victory in these debates. Over time, as slavery gradually was abolished, a systematic network of attitudes and practices based on the concept of race evolved across all fields and activities of New World societies with a uniquely pervasive, saturating force. The primary purpose of this racialized thinking was, under the guise of different vocabularies, to rationalize and maintain in public and private spheres the power European slave owners once held over their African slaves.

Emmett Till was murdered because he violated taboos governing race relations in 1955 in Money, a rural Mississippi town, but his killers were also exercising and revalidating prerogatives in place since their ancestors imported Emmett Till's ancestors to these shores. At some level everybody in Money understood this. Our horror, our refusal to look too closely at Emmett Till reside in the same deep, incriminating knowledge.

Perhaps an apartheid mentality reigns in this country because most Americans consciously hold racist attitudes or wish ill on their neighbors of African descent. I don't think so. Emmett Till dies again and again because his murder, the conditions that ensure and perpetuate it have not been honestly examined. Denial is more acceptable to the majority of Americans than placing themselves, their inherited dominance, at risk.

Any serious attempt to achieve economic, social and political equal opportunity in this nation must begin not simply with opening doors to selected minorities. That impulse, that trope, that ideology has failed. The majority must decide to relinquish significant measures of power and privilege if lasting transformations of self and society are to occur. There have always been open doors of sorts for minorities (emancipation, emigration, education, economic success in sports or business, passing as white). What's missing is an unambiguous, abiding determination declared in public and private by a majority of the majority to surrender privileges that are the living legacy of slavery. Begin now. Today. Give up walls, doors, keys, the dungeons, the booty, the immunity, the false identity apartheid preserves.

A first step is acknowledging that the dangerous lies of slavery continue to be told as long as we conceive of ourselves in terms of race, as black or white.

Emmett Till and the young victims of drug and territory wars raging in African-American neighborhoods today are signs of a deeply flawed society failing its children. Why do we perceive the bodies of dead *black* boys, imprisoned *black* men, homeless *black* people, addicted *black* people as *black* problems? Why do we support cynical politicians who cite these *black* problems as evidence for more brutal policing of the racial divide?

In 1955, one year after the Supreme Court's Brown v. Board of Education school-desegregation decision, a great struggle for civil rights commenced. The lynching of Emmett Till should have clarified exactly what was at stake: life or death. As long as racialized thinking continues to legitimize one group's life-and-death power over another, the battered face of Emmett Till will poison the middle ground of compromise between so-called "whites" and so-called "blacks." His face unmourned, unburied, unloved, haunting the netherworld where incompatible versions of democracy clash.

It was hard to bury Emmett Till, hard, hard to bury Carole Robertson, Addie Mae Collins, Denise McNair and Cynthia Wesley, the four girls killed by a bomb in a Birmingham, Ala., church. So hard an entire nation began to register the convulsions of black mourning. The deaths of our children in the civil-rights campaigns changed us. The oratory of great men like Martin Luther King Jr. pushed us to realize our grief should be collective, should stir us to unify, to clarify our thinking, roll back the rock of fear. Emmett Till's mangled face could belong to anybody's son who transgressed racial laws; anyone's little girl could be crushed in the rubble of a bombed church. We read the terrorist threat inscribed upon Emmett Till's flesh and were shaken but refused to comply with the terrorists' demands.

Martin Luther King Jr. understood the killing of our children was an effort to murder the nation's future. We mourned the young martyrs, and a dedicated few risked life and limb fighting with ferocity and dignity in the courts, churches and streets to stop the killing. Young people served as shock troops in the movement for social justice, battling on the front lines, the hottest, most dangerous spots in Alabama and Mississippi. And though they had most to gain or lose (their precious lives, their time on this earth), they also carried on their shoulders the hopes of older generations and generations unborn.

Now there seems to be in our rituals of mourning for our dying children no sense of communal, general loss, no larger, empowering vision. We don't connect our immediate trials—drugs, gang violence, empty schools, empty minds, empty homes, empty values—to the ongoing, historical struggle to liberate ourselves from the oppressive legacies of slavery and apartheid. Funerals for our young are lonely occurrences. Daily it seems, in some ghetto or another somewhere in America, a small black congregation will gather together to try to repair the hole in a brother's or mother's soul with the balm of gospel singing, prayer, the laying on of dark hands on darkened spirits.

How many a week, how many repetitions of the same, sad, isolated ceremony, the hush afterward when the true dimensions of loss and futility begin to set in? A sense of futility, of powerlessness dogs the survivors, who are burdened not only by the sudden death of a loved one but also by the knowledge that it's going to happen again today or tomorrow and that it's supposed to happen in a world where black lives are expendable, can disappear, *click*, in a fingerpop, quick like that, without a trace, as if the son or sister was hardly here at all. Hey, maybe black people really ain't worth shit, just like you've been hearing your whole life.

Curtis Jones, a cousin who accompanied Emmett Till on the trip from Chicago, Ill., to Money, Miss., in August 1955, relates how close Emmett Till came to missing their train, reminding us how close Emmett Till's story came to not happening or being another story altogether, and that in turn should remind us how any story, sad or happy, is always precariously close to being other than it is. Doesn't take much to alter a familiar scene into chaos. Difficult as it is to remember what does occur, we must also try to keep alive what doesn't—the missed trains, squandered opportunities, warnings not heeded. We carry forward these fictions because what might have been is part of what gives shape to our stories. We depend on memory's capacity to hold many lives, not just the one we appear to be leading at the moment. Memory is space for storing lives we didn't lead, room where they remain alive, room for mourning them, forgiving them. Memory, like all stories we tell, a tissue of remembering, forgetting, of *what if* and *once upon a time*, burying our dead so the dead may rise.

Curtis Jones goes on to tell us about everybody piling into Grandpa Wright's automobile and trundling down the dusty road to church. How he and his cousin Emmett Till took the car into Money that afternoon while Moses Wright preached.

A bunch of boys loafing outside Bryant's General Store on Money's main drag. Sho 'nuff country town. Wooden storefronts with wooden porches. Wooden sidewalks. Overhanging wooden signs. With its smatter of brown boys out front, its frieze of tire-sized Coca-Cola signs running around the eaves of its porch, Bryant's the only game in town, Emmett Till guessed.

Climbing out of Moses Wright's old Dodge, he sports the broad smile I recall from another photo, the one of him leaning, elbow atop a TV set, clean as a string bean in his white dress shirt and tie, his chest thrust out mannishly, baby fat in his cheeks, a softish, still-forming boy whose energy, intelligence and expectations of life are evident in the pose he's striking for the camera, just enough in-your-face swagger that you can't help smiling back at the wary eagerness to please of his smile.

To Emmett Till the boys in Money's streets are a cluster of down-home country cousins. He sees a stage beckoning on which he can perform. Steps up on the sidewalk with his cousin Curtis, to whom he is *Bo* or *Bobo*, greets his audience. Like a magician pulling a rabbit from his hat, Emmett Till pulls a white girl from his wallet. Silences everybody. Mesmerizes them with tales of what they're missing, living down here in the Mississippi woods. If he'd been selling magic beans, all of them would have dug into their overalls and extracted their last, hot penny to buy some. They watch his fingers slip into his shirt pocket. Hold their breath waiting for the next trick.

Emmett Till's on a roll, can't help rubbing it in a little. What he's saying about himself sounds real good, so good he wants to hear more. All he wants really is for these brown faces to love him. As much as he's loved by the dark faces and light faces in the junior-high graduation pictures from Chicago he's showing around.

He winks at the half-dozen or so boys gathered round him. Nods. Smiles like the cat swallowed the canary. Points to the prettiest girl, the fairest, longest-haired one of all you can easily see, even though the faces in the class picture are tiny and gray. Emmett Till says she is the prettiest, anyway, so why not? Why not believe he's courted and won her, and ain't you-all lucky he come down here bringing you-all the good news?

Though Emmett Till remains the center of attention, the other kids giggle, scratch their naps, stroke their chins, turn their heads this way and that around the circle, commence little conversations of eye-cutting and teeth-sucking and slack-jawed awe. Somebody pops a finger against somebody's shaved skull. Somebody's hip bumps somebody else. A tall boy whistles a blues line, and you notice someone's been humming softly the whole time. Emmett Till's the preacher, and it's Sunday morning, and the sermon is righteous. On the other hand, everybody's ready for a hymn or a responsive reading, even a collection plate circulating, so they can participate, stretch their bones, hear their own voices.

You sure is something, boy. You say you bad, Emmett Till. Got all them white gals up North, you say. Bet you won't say boo to the white lady in the store.

Curtis Jones is playing checkers with old Uncle Edmund on a barrel set in the shade around the corner from the main drag. One of the boys who sauntered into the store with Emmett Till to buy candy comes running. *He did it. Emmett Till did it. That cousin of yours crazy, boy. Said, "Bye-bye, Baby," to Miss Bryant.*

The old man gets up so fast he knocks over the crate he's been sitting on. *Lor' have mercy. I know the boy didn't do nothing like that. Huh-uh. No. No, he didn't. You-all better get out here. That lady come out that store blow you-all's brains off.*

Several months later, after an all-white jury in the town of Sumner, Miss., had deliberated an hour— *Would have been less if we hadn't took time for lunch*—and found Roy Bryant and J.W. Milam not guilty of murdering Emmett Till, the two men were paid $4,000 by a journalist, William Bradford Huie, to tell the story of abducting, beating and shooting Emmett Till.

To get rid of his body, they barbwired a 50-pound cotton-gin fan to Emmett Till's neck and threw him in the Tallahatchie River. The journalist, in a videotaped interview, said, "It seems to a rational mind today—it seems impossible that they could have killed him."

The reporter muses for a moment, then remembers, "But J.W. Milam looked up at me, and he says, 'Well, when he told me about this white girl he had, my friend, well, that's what this war's about down here now, that's what we got to fight to protect, and I just looked at him and say, *Boy, you ain't never gone to see the sun come up again.*'"

To the very end, Emmett Till didn't believe the crackers would kill him. He was 14, from Chicago. He'd hurt no one. These strange, funny-talking white men were a nightmare he'd awaken from sooner or later. Milam found the boy's lack of fear shocking. Called it "belligerence." Here was this nigger should be shitting his drawers. Instead he was making J.W. Milam uncomfortable. Brave or foolhardy or ignorant or blessed to be already in another place, a place these sick, sick men could never touch, whatever enabled Emmett Till to stand his ground, to be himself until the first deadly blow landed, be himself even after it landed, I hope Emmett Till understood that Milam or Bryant, whoever struck first with the intent to kill, was the one who flinched, not him.

When such thoughts come to me, I pile them like sandbags along the levees that protect my sleep. I should know better than to waste my time.

In another dream we emerge at dawn from the tree line. Breeze into Money. Rat-tat. Rat-tat-tat. Waste the whole motherfucking ville. Nothing to it. Little hick town 'bout same today as when they lynched poor brother Emmett Till.

Some the bitches come rubbing up against us after we lined 'em up by the ditch. Thinking maybe if they fuck us they won't die. We let 'em try. You know. Wasn't bad pussy, neither. But when the time come, you know, they got to go just like the rest. Rat-tat-tat. Uh-huh.

Money gone. Burnt a hole in its pocket.

I asked a lover, a woman whose whiteness made her a flesh-and-blood embodiment of the nightmare J.W. Milam discovered in Emmett Till's wallet, what she thinks of when she hears "Emmett Till."

"A black kid whistling at a white woman somewhere down South and being killed for it, is what I think," she said.

"He didn't whistle," I reply. I've heard the wolf-whistle story all my life and another that has him not moving aside for a white woman walking down the sidewalk. Both are part of the myth, but neither's probably true. The story Till's cousin Curtis Jones tells is different. And for what it's worth, his cousin was there. Something Emmett Till said to a white woman inside a store is what started it.

She wants to know where I heard the cousin's version, and I launch into a riff on my sources—"Voices of Freedom," an oral history of the civil rights movement; Henry Hampton's video documentary, "Eyes on the Prize"; a book, "Representations of Black Masculinity in Contemporary American Art," organized around a museum exhibit of black male images. Then I realize I'm doing all the talking, when what I'd intended to elicit was her spontaneous witness. What her memory carried forward, what it lost.

She's busy with something of her own, and we just happened to cross paths a moment in the kitchen, and she's gone before I get what I wanted. Gone before I know what I wanted. Except standing there next to the refrigerator, in the silence released by its hum, I feel utterly defeated. All the stuff spread out on my desk isn't getting me any closer to Emmett Till or a cure. Neither will man-in-the-street, woman-in-the-kitchen interviews. Other people's facts and opinions don't matter. Only one other person's voice required for this story I'm constructing to overcome a bad dream, and they shut him up a long time ago, didn't they?

Here is what happened. Four nights after the candy-buying and "Bye-bye, Baby" scene in Money, at 2 a.m. on August 21, 1955, Roy Bryant, with a pistol in one hand and a flashlight in the other, appears at Moses Wright's door. "This is Mr. Bryant," he calls into the darkness. Then demands to know if Moses Wright has two niggers from Chicago inside. He says he wants the nigger done all that talk.

When Emmett Till is delivered, Bryant marches him to a car and asks someone inside, "This the right nigger?" and somebody says, "Yes, he is."

Next time Moses Wright sees Emmett Till is three days later when the sheriff summons him to identify a corpse. The body's naked and too badly damaged to tell who it is until Moses Wright notices the initialed ring on his nephew's finger.

Where were you when JFK was shot? Where were you when a man landed on the moon? When Martin Luther King Jr. was shot? Malcolm shot? When the Rodney King verdict announced? Where were you when Emmett Till floated up to the surface of the Tallahatchie River for *Bye-bye Baby*ing a white woman?

A white man in the darkness outside a tarpaper cabin announcing the terror of his name, gripping a flashlight in his fist, a heavy-duty flashlight stuffed with thick, D batteries that will become a club for bashing Emmett Till's skull.

An old black man in the shanty crammed with bodies, instantly alert when he hears, "You got those niggers from Chicago in there with you?" An old man figuring the deadly odds, how many lives bought if one handed over. Calculating the rage of his ancient enemy, weighing the risk of saying what he wants the others in his charge to hear, Emmett Till to hear, no matter what terrible things happen next.

"Got my two grandsons and a nephew in here."

A black boy inside the cabin, a boy my age whose name I don't know yet, who will never know mine. He rubs his eyes, not sure he's awake or dreaming a scary dream, one of the tales buried deep, deep he's been hearing since before we were born about the old days in the Deep South when they cut off niggers' nuts and lynched niggers and roasted niggers over fires like marshmallows.

A man in my own, warm bed, lying beside a beautiful woman rubbing my shoulder, a pale, blond woman whose presence sometimes is as strange and unaccountable to me as mine must be to her, as snow falling softly through the bedroom ceiling would be, accumulating in white drifts on the down comforter.

Why am I telling Emmett Till's story this way, attempting the miracle or cheap trick of being many people, many places at once? Will words change what happened, what's missing, what's lost? Will my nightmare dissolve if I cling to the woman almost asleep now next to me, end if I believe this loving moment together might last and last?

The name *Emmett* is spoiled for me. In any of its spellings. As big a kick as I get from watching Emmitt Smith rush the football for the Dallas Cowboys, there is also the moment after a bone-shattering collision and he's sprawled lifeless on the turf or the moment after he's stumbled or fumbled and slumps to the bench and lifts his helmet and I see a black mother's son, a small, dark, round face, a boy's big, wide, scared eyes. All those yards gained, all that wealth, but like O.J. he'll never run far enough or fast enough. Inches behind him the worst thing the people who hate him can imagine hounds him like a shadow.

Sometimes I think the only way to end this would be with Andy Warhol-like strips of images, the same face, Emmett Till's face, replicated 12, 24, 48, 96 times on a wall-sized canvas. Like giant postage stamps end to end, top to bottom, each version of the face exactly like the other but different names printed below each one. Martin Luther Till. Malcolm Till. Medgar Till. Nat Till. Gabriel Till. Michael Till. Huey Till. Bigger Till. Nelson Till. Mumia Till. Colin Till. Jesse Till. Your daddy, your mama, your sister, brother, aunt, cousin, uncle, niece, nephew Till...

Instead of the nightmare one night, this is what I dream.

I'm marching with many, many men, a multitude, a million men of all colors in Washington, D.C., marching past the bier on which the body of Emmett Till rests. The casket, as his mother demanded, is open. *I want the world to see what they did to my baby.* One by one from an endless line, the men detach themselves, pause, peer down into the satin-lined box. Pinned inside its upright lid a snapshot of Emmett Till, young, smiling, whole, a jaunty Stetson cocked high across his brow. In the casket Emmett Till is dressed in a dark suit, jacket wings spread to expose a snowy shroud pulled up to his chin. Then the awful face, patched together with string and wire, awaits each mourner.

My turn is coming soon. I'm grateful. Will not shy away this time. Will look hard this time. The line of my brothers and fathers and sons stretches ahead of me, behind me. I am drawn by them, pushed by them, steadied as we move each other along. We are a horizon girding the earth, holding the sky down. So many of us in one place at one time it scares me. More than a million of us marching through this city of monumental buildings and dark alleys. Not very long ago, we were singing, but now we march silently, more shuffle than brisk step as we approach the bier, wait our turn. Singing's over, but it holds silently in the air, tangible as weather, as the bright sun disintegrating marble buildings, emptying alleys of shadows, warming us on a perfect October day we had no right to expect but would have been profoundly disappointed had it fallen out otherwise.

What I say when I lean over and speak one last time to Emmett Till is *I love you. I'm sorry. I won't allow it to happen ever again.* And my voice will be small and quiet when I say the words, not nearly as humble as it should be, fearful almost to pledge any good after so much bad. My small voice and short turn, and then the next man and the next, close together, leading, following one another so the murmur of our voices beside the bier never stops. An immensity, a continuous, muted shout and chant and benediction, a river gliding past the stillness of Emmett Till. Past this city, this hour, this place. River sound of blood I'm almost close enough to hear coursing in the veins of the next man.

In the dream we do not say, *Forgive us.* We are taking, not asking for something today. There is no time left to ask for things, even things as precious as forgiveness, only time to take one step, then the next and the next, alone in this great body of men, each one standing on his own feet, moving, our shadows linked, a coolness, a shield stretching nearly unbroken across the last bed where Emmett Till sleeps.

Where we bow and hope and pray he frees us. Ourselves seen, sinking, then rising as in a mirror, then stepping away.

And then. And then this vision fades, too. I am there and not there. Not in Washington, D.C., marching with a million other men. My son Dan, my new granddaughter Qasima's father, marched. He was a witness, and the arc of his witness includes me as mine, his. So, yes, I was there in a sense but not there to view the face of Emmett Till because Emmett Till was not there, either, not in an open casket displayed to the glory of the heavens, the glories of this republic, not there except as a shadow, a stain, a wound in the million faces of the marchers, the faces of their absent fathers, sons and brothers.

We have yet to look upon Emmett Till's face. No apocalyptic encounter, no ritual unveiling, no epiphany has freed us. The nightmare is not cured.

I cannot wish away Emmett Till's face. The horrific death mask of his erased features marks a site I ignore at my peril. The site of a grievous wound. A wound unhealed because untended. Beneath our nation's pieties, our self-delusions, our denials and distortions of history, our professed black-and-white certainties about race, lies chaos. The whirlwind that swept Emmett Till away and brings him back.

__John Edgar Wideman__'s life is as dramatic as any of his widely acclaimed Faulknerian novels. Born in Pittsburgh to a working-class family, he became the second African-American Rhodes Scholar and a college basketball star, as talented on the court as he was brilliant in the classroom. He is the first writer to win the PEN/Faulkner Award twice, in 1984 for "See You Yesterday" and in 1990 for "Philadelphia Fire." His nonfiction book, "Brothers and Keepers," received a National Book Critics Circle nomination, and his memoir, "Fatheralong," was a finalist for the National Book Award. His most recent book, "Hoop Roots," is a memoir. He is a professor of creative writing at the University of Massachusetts at Amherst and a columnist for New York Times Book Review.

Snapshots in Black and White

Shara McCallum

*M*y father died when I was 9 years old, the same year my three sisters and my mother moved with our mother's parents to America, to Miami. He was mixed: African, Indian, European (from Scotland and England), Jewish and we don't know what else. He had schizophrenia. Schizophrenia, a metaphor for multiple selves.

What I remember of my father are fragments. I see him with his guitar. I see him singing and strumming his guitar. I see myself next to him in the gully in his mother's back yard with him playing and singing to me. I see him frozen on a busy street in Kingston: catatonic. I see him cursing and screaming and hitting my mother: paranoid, delusional. I see him crying at his reflection in the mirror.

My father was a Rastafarian for the last 10 years of his life, and my three sisters and I, born in Jamaica, were raised as Rastas, too. My mother tells me that, as a youth, my father went to England and later studied Buddhism before coming to Rastafari, in attempts to understand who he was. By the end of his life, though, he considered himself a black man, she says. "He had gone deep into himself to reach that point and make himself whole." Whole. Schizophrenia. My father tried to commit suicide many times. He succeeded at 33. Schizophrenia is not a metaphor. Race is not a metaphor.

The first time I meet anyone who has known me before seeing me is always the most difficult and uncomfortable moment for each of us: editors who have published my work, someone who has seen my resumé without a picture. The usual blank stare for a moment. The stuttering *"You* are Shara McCallum."

For many years, in part to avoid this sting, in part out of fear of going against the grain, of rocking the boat, I checked "Other" or wrote "mixed" and listed the four continents to which I can lay claim within the span of two generations. A mutt. Mulatta. High yella. Miscegenated. Mixed breed. A dog. A nectarine.

As a child in Jamaica, I was not oblivious to color. I knew I had white or bright or light skin while others had brown and yellow and beige and red and black—cool brown, doo-doo brown, light as light, cream with a dash of coffee, coffee with a dash of cream, reds, lick of the tar brush, coal black, black as night. But I did not understand the usual intersections of color and race. When we came to America, I didn't know that I was black or white. I was 9 and trying to be like the other kids, trying to lose my accent and sound American, trying to catch up on TV shows I'd missed since we didn't have a TV back home in Jamaica, trying to learn to play with Barbie dolls when before I had cooked and cleaned for my younger sisters, trying to learn to wear Chic jeans and feel chic after not having been allowed to wear pants up to that point in my life. I didn't know I was black until my grandmother, my mother's mother, told me, "No one would ever know you are. Only your hair might give you away." Then it became a secret. Something to be mentioned only among us, if even that.

I have six sisters. Three are from my mother and father and are, like me, able to "pass." Of those, one chooses not to acknowledge any ancestry other than European. One acknowledges her other blood but considers herself white. The last one identifies herself as black and Hispanic, our mother being Venezuelan-Jamaican. Of my other three sisters, one is from my father and another woman before I was born; two are the children of my mother and another man, after my father died. All three are visibly mixed, with anything from Indian to Venezuelan to Chinese to British and African ancestry, but all three are still visibly black. I have six sisters. We all share parts of the same genetic codes.

Breaking the silence is not easy. There is no good way to tell someone you are black when you look white. If they are black, the worst scenario is that they will think you are putting them on or condescending to them or crazy or lying. If they are white, they will think you are crazy.

My aunt is Hispanic or white by U.S. standards of race, but she identifies herself as "Other" when she has to check the boxes. She says she is Jamaican. She is also a lesbian. When I am in college, I ask her what it's like to live as a lesbian, and she responds first that the word makes her uncomfortable. She prefers *gay*. It sounds less harsh. When she meets people for the first time who don't know she is gay, she has to be careful, she says, and on guard for what they might say. Depending on the circumstances, she adds, she cannot be found out.

I have lived in East Meredith for almost a year when this happens. Steve and I have moved from Maryland, outside of Washington, D.C., to a rural town in upstate New York. We live on a dirt road with cows half a mile away in any direction. I go to the post office two or three times a week, and John, the postmaster, knows me by name. Every time I come in, he chirps hello, smiles, and comments, "You've been busy." Today I tell him that two letters to home—one to my aunt, the other to my sister—have never reached them. He says it's not on this end but probably all those Hispanics and blacks in Miami who just take up space and don't do their jobs. I have known him for 11 months. Faced with his remark, I cannot find my voice. I leave in shame and stunned silence. We are moving to another small town in a few weeks, but to avoid seeing him again, I drive half an hour to the post office in the next town.

I tell this story to a militant "sistuh" I barely know because she will see me as a coward and I need her censure. She does not disappoint, looks at me and sneers. "It is your responsibility to speak and fight every time, *especially* since you can pass." I say nothing to her, either. I don't tell her of the time in Conyers, Ga., in that place where it is supposed to happen, where you go expecting to hear it, that I went against my friend's pleas, my friend who had taken me to her home town, and I stood up to a burly white man who said "nigger," who looked as if he would strike me down when I spoke back. I don't tell her that sometimes, it is also hard to admit, I am tired of it all.

My grandmother considers herself white but also West Indian and maybe even British, England being the "mother country" from which she was adopted and brought to Trinidad to be raised. Most of all, she says, "I am human." My grandfather, by right if not biology, is her second husband, a Jamaican man who is also visibly mixed—his mother a light-skinned black woman, his father a Portuguese Jew. In Miami strangers automatically speak to him in Spanish, assuming he is Cuban. My grandmother delights in the looks on these strangers' faces when she, a white-skinned, blond-haired, blue-eyed woman—who lived in Venezuela for 12 years—answers in perfect Spanish, *"El no habla español. Me ayuda?"*

Passing is the ability to go between or the inability to take root. Race is the desire to take root or the forcing to take root that which could otherwise go between.

Like my aunt, her sister—my mother—does not like the "boxes." She tells me that she checks whichever ones she is in the mood to check that day. Often, she says, she checks them all, "just to fuck with them."

My mother has been a Rastafarian since she was 18 years old. She turned 46 this June. When I was growing up, I did not know it then, but I was learning that *white* meant Babylon, meant imperialism, economic privilege, racial and foreign domination, oppression. Whether she looks white or not, my mother says, she has fought against that type of whiteness her whole life. She has fought against and within her own skin.

Sometimes my skin feels as if it wants to burst into flames. Sometimes I wish it were a coat I could take off. Sometimes I look at it and see the proof of my life and my frequent, shameful desire to live outside of the body. Sometimes I look at it and see the proof of my life and my constant need to accept and live within this body. Sometimes I look at it and see one of my great-great-grandmothers, the mistress with whip in her hand. Sometimes through my aloe-colored eyes, I see another of my great-great-grandmothers, back arched against the curve of that lash.

*Born in Jamaica, **Shara McCallum** immigrated to the United States at the age of 9. Her book of poetry, "The Water Between Us," won the Agnes Lynch Starrett Prize in 1998 and was published in 1999. McCallum has published poems and essays in the Antioch Review, Chelsea, Iowa Review, Witness and elsewhere. She lives in Memphis, Tenn., and teaches in the master of fine arts program at the University of Memphis.*

Joe Stopped By

Andrei Codrescu

*W*hen I handed her the phone, Laura looked like I was taking her to the dentist. Her father was in town and threatened to come over. I had met the guy twice. The first time we stood on the lawn of Laura's old place on Myrtledale, and he looked on me suspiciously, like he must have looked on all her boyfriends since she started bringing them home around the age of 16. He complained about his truck and the lack of rain on his pecan trees, and I told him that the publishing industry was going to the dogs. Nice conversation. Mutual incomprehension. Lasted about five minutes.

Next time I had the pleasure of Joe's company was the day after Christmas. He called and said that he'd be over in two hours. We had just cleaned up after the Christmas dinner the night before. Laura's mother, Laura's two sons, and a couple of friends had come over to eat. We were still hung over, and there were a lot of dirty dishes. The timing wasn't great. Two hours later, Joe showed up with his wife, Carolyn; Laura's sister, Susan; Susan's husband, Lloyd; and Susan's daughter. Joe plunked himself down in an armchair in the front room and declared the excesses of Christmas bankrupt and insufficiently mindful of Christ. Carolyn, who agreed with everything her husband said, added that in their church people were against materialism and that godless TV was turned off during the holidays so people can have a nice, non-alcoholic dinner and praise the Lord. They lived in Jigger, a small town in northern Louisiana near the Mississippi border. They had moved there after Joe's second triple-bypass surgery. He'd given up his wife, drink, cigarettes and the law and taken up Carolyn, Jesus and farming. He'd been a prosecutor in West Baton Rouge Parish and a ward heeler for Dixiecrats running for state offices. He gave up all that.

The Christmas visit wasn't so bad because Joe was kind of hemmed in between Laura and Susan and couldn't express himself very clearly. His daughters knew him too well and anticipated nearly every one of his yarns with a detouring quip. And then there was Carolyn. Once Carolyn's shrill voice launched forth the battleship of a story, there was no stopping her. She churned the waves at top speed, and there was nothing anyone could do except get out of the way and let the parable subside. Her stories were all parables. One of her sons had bad grades for a year; then he found himself and did well. The moral of that was that everybody has their own timetable. That was a placating parable for liberals like me, offered in penance for one of Joe's unfinished stories about educational problems among the darker-skinned folk. Joe's story had been ruthlessly chopped to pieces by the whirring blades of Laura and Susan's daddy-choppers, but Carolyn figured that enough of it had gotten out to offend the liberal establishment—me.

Joe had seen action in Japan and wasn't going to buy anything Japanese if his life depended on it. "I'd rather shave with broken glass than the best Toyota shaver they got," he announced. That was how far he got that time in the land of diversity. His daughters were quick to point out that you couldn't tell the difference anymore between what the Japanese and the Americans made, because they were all mixed up together, from management to actual parts in cars and electronics. That nearly got him, because if there was anything he couldn't abide, it was this mixing. He had views on that and on miscegenation, but they never saw the light of day. His girls saw to that.

After they left we felt a residual weirdness, like another kind of hangover. We tried to analyze it. He had gotten Laura all worked up, which was, she said, "his specialty." The former prosecutor had been a formidable dinner-table presence in her childhood. She had honed fearsome debating skills to resist the onslaught of her father's provocations. He had used the family as practice for the court. They all felt like lawyers and criminals, always on the alert for another burst of eloquence, sure to be defeated but not allowed to give up before putting up a good fight. Laura's mother had reacted by creating a passive-aggressive resistance that was intricate, mute and so "feminine" the prosecutor couldn't get in. It was like going into a women's bathroom. He was a gentleman. He drew the line there. His daughters adopted different strategies. Susan also played the feminine card and wriggled and winked and brought up matters of esoteric hormonal import that were worse than trespassing into the ladies' room. Joe flirted with her for self-preservation. Laura, on the other hand, met him head on, on his own turf. She countered and parried his arguments, got the better of him, didn't quit until he admitted defeat, which he never did. Outside the home Joe played rough and dirty for his candidates. Laura went after him in the field. She played dirty. She seduced daddy's law partner. She was only 15. When Joe found out, he was ready to shoot somebody, but who was he going to shoot? He made a lot of belligerent noises. Did he admit defeat? No. He had a heart attack instead. Left her mother. Took up Jesus. Well, not in that order, but this was the order that Laura saw at the time. No amount of grown-up reason could later dislodge it. She'd felt personally responsible for all the disasters subsequent to her victory, and it had put her in an untenable position. She learned that victory over daddy is a terrible thing but that daddies can be defeated using female wiles. Her insurgent sexuality was a match for any man's posturing, including her invincible daddy's. Is there a worse thing to learn in your adolescence? Of course the sonofabitch had invited it. He had challenged and challenged, prodded and poked until she had gotten her back up. Was he surprised? Of course. It had been only a game for him. He never expected to be taken seriously.

On the other hand, I'm a man. How am I supposed to take this? Here I am living with a woman who is both a skilled debater and a guilt-ridden daddy-killer. I say guilt-ridden because that is what I attribute her extreme sensitivity to. Laura under attack is a lot like an aroused lynx. She did in the king; who am I to oppose her? But her guilt is also her weakness. If she makes too bold a move, she throws herself, weeping, into my arms. I hold her there; then I seduce her. She gives all of herself. She never wanted anything else. She only wanted daddy to admit defeat and then hold her. I never admit defeat, but I hold her. I am a man, just like her daddy, but I cannot be killed because I am her lover, like her daddy's enemy whom she seduced at 15. I am both daddy and anti-daddy. We get along just fine.

The third time Joe came to visit, he gave no more notice than he did before. But there was something different this time, and he made a mistake being casual. Laura and I had gotten married the month before. Joe knew, but he didn't say a word. He didn't call or write the whole month. And now he was coming over on two hours' notice.

Carolyn was right behind him, chatty like a sparrow on a fence-post. Joe made a dash toward the commanding post of the first arm-chair, but I beat him to it. He had to sit next to his daughter on the couch. Carolyn took the other armchair. Between us was a table, on which sat a fine chess set with figures that looked sculpted by Brancusi, my co-national, who made ovoids. It was a birthday present from Laura. Carolyn showed off the carved ivory piece around her neck. She had matching earrings.

"An ivory orchid," said Laura. "Isn't ivory illegal?"

"It's fossil ivory!" gloated Carolyn. "My friend found it in Canada and had the craftsman carve it into an orchid. It's a birthday present from Joe."

Laura pointed to the chess set. "That's my birthday present to Andrei."

"Do you play chess?" Joe asked, as if he was asking if I was homosexual.

"Yes," I said. "The best chess players are in jail and in Eastern Europe."

"Five-year-old Hungarian girls!" Laura said. "Masters."

"The only thing I'd know to do with a chess set is take out my gun and shoot the queen," said Joe.

"That wouldn't be very useful," I said.

Carolyn sensed danger. "Did you see it snowed in Shreveport at New Year's? We were at the church playing dominoes after the New Year's meal and heard the radio announce snow, so everybody went home. The kids were disappointed."

"Our people," Joe said, "the Scotch-Irish, Anglo-Saxon people…"

Laura was ready. Carolyn was ready. I was waiting.

"Our people," Joe said, enjoying the suspense, "have a whiskey problem, so the preachers and the bootleggers got together and declared the town dry. In the old days, women couldn't walk down the main street without being shouted at. There were gunfights. They outlawed it, and the drinking moved outside the town limits. Jigger is peaceful now."

Everybody laughed. What a relief. Joe was being self-mocking. Then he sighed and said, "Burnt cork! Burnt cork!"

"Yes," he continued when he saw bafflement, "the dark-skinned ones all got $50,000 from the government because they were discriminated on past loans. I need to get some burnt cork to rub my face with and get myself $50,000, too."

"We don't have enough money for our seniors' hot-meal program," said Carolyn, as if there was a connection.

Joe said that the two counties, theirs and the neighboring one, received unequal money for the seniors' program, even though they were exactly the same size. When I asked why, Joe said it was because of the two representatives in the state house in Baton Rouge. One got the money; the other didn't.

I stared at the chess set. I didn't want to know what colors these representatives were. Joe didn't push it.

"Did you hear about that county in Florida—Palm Beach, I think it was—where they tried to make Spanish mandatory? They were going to outlaw English."

"Like in Quebec," agreed Carolyn.

"Indeed," said Joe, "Carolyn won't eat in any of those damn restaurants in Quebec. If they can't print their menus in English, no do-re-mi for you!"

"Too bad," I said. "You'll be missing some fine French food. We eat from French-only menus right here in Baton Rouge. Paté. Croissants. Etouffé. Sauté."

"That county in Florida," Joe said, "where they had all those poor illiterates—that's where they tried to outlaw English."

"My mother lives there," I said, "and her English is fine."

"And she didn't vote for Buchanan, that's for sure," laughed Laura. "She voted for Gore."

"They showed that Florida ballot in a nursing home in New York. Everybody figured it out. One woman said, 'They've been out in the sun too long in Florida.'" Joe stopped to laugh to himself and lifted his hand, warning of the coming of a joke. "They asked Barbara Bush why people thought Dubya wasn't too smart, and she said, 'Who's smarter? Dubya, who has an M.B.A. from Harvard, or Gore, who dropped out of divinity school?'"

Joe and Carolyn laughed. We did, too. Laura said, "Gore left divinity school to go to Vietnam. And no mother's going to say her son is dumb. We are still waiting to see how dumb he is."

"Nobody goes to divinity school," I said, "to make good grades. They go there to think about serious issues."

"I went to get an eye exam in Florida," Joe said, "and the optician was a retired Canadian who had sold seven optical shops in Canada before he retired. He couldn't stay put, so he built himself another one in Palm Beach. He couldn't stand it, he said, because of all those whiny, pushy New York Jews. He was moving back to Canada."

"That's just how they are—pushy," agreed Carolyn.

"He couldn't have been a very good optician because nobody could read that spaghetti ballot," I said. Some of my good humor was beginning to fray around the edges. So far Joe had gone after nearly everything he suspected I was: a Jew, a liberal, a Spanish-speaking something...but of course there was more. In our three encounters so far, he had not asked me once where I was from. I would have told him. Transylvania. Southern Romania. Ex-commie country. He knew all that but not from me. When Carolyn said later, "You're a teacher. You know what I mean," apropos of something or other, I realized that of all my identities and possible places of origin, they had settled on "teacher" as the least offensive. A teacher might marry Joe's daughter, but all those other things—ex-commies, writers, Transylvanians— they had no right.

"It can be argued," Joe said in a sort of prosecutorial manner that had Laura half out of her seat, "that the Southern states are still under occupation."

"By whom, pray," laughed his daughter, "with a Southerner in the White House, and a Republican congress?"

"By the armies of Northern aggression..." Joe intoned gravely.

"That would be Wal-Mart," I said.

"Yup," agreed Laura, "occupied by Sam Walton."

Carolyn thought that it was time to intervene for reasons of balance. "I hate Wal-Mart," she said. "We had a nice little store with every- thing—children's, women's, men's. It's gone now. There was another little store one town over. Gone. Wal-Mart's the only store in 50 miles."

"The bankers are bankrupting the farmers," said Joe. "The New York bankers."

Carolyn followed on the footsteps of that with a detailed account of the disasters wrought on farmers by Wall Street. Their own 35 acres of pecans were not in question; the soul of the country was.

"Where is all that booming economy Bill Clinton was talking about? I don't see any money." Joe looked angry.

For once I agreed with him. "It's funny how that booming economy left with Clinton."

"Everybody around Clinton dies mysteriously," Joe said, having had enough of making nice. "Just like that. They found a guy shot in the back of the head. They said it was suicide."

"Must be the Kennedy syndrome," Laura said.

"That was the work of a single gunman," Joe said proudly. "That Jackie Kennedy was one loose woman."

"Her children were probably all by Jack's daddy, Joe," Laura sighed, briefly amused by the game.

Joe laughed, but Carolyn didn't.

I wondered who was left. We had already done the Japanese the first time we met. The Jews, the Hispanics, the Quebecois and the Catholics had just been disposed of. Joe was in a good mood.

"When Earl K. Long couldn't run for governor anymore, he ran a friend of his. They were campaigning in northern Louisiana, and Earl went to take a leak in the bushes while his man, who was a terrible speaker, kept droning on and on. When Earl came back, an old-timer who didn't understand one word of the speech said, 'Is that guy a communiss?' Earl laughed. 'No,' he said, 'he's a Catholic. He can't be a communiss; his brother is a priest.' 'I knew there was sumpthin',' the old man said."

We all laughed, Carolyn the loudest. She was Catholic.

Joe got suddenly serious. "I first voted in 1948. I didn't vote for either Truman or Dewey. I voted for Strom Thurmond. He was running on states' rights."

"A lot of elections since then," I said. "I wish I understood what Strom says when he speaks."

"Sure," Joe said. "How about that Jesse Jackson? Is he going to retire with Jimmy Swaggart and that Tammy Faye Bakker?"

He was being conciliatory. I extended a finger, too. "I can't understand what Jesse Jackson says, either."

"They should have a conversation, Strom and Jesse," laughed Laura.

Joe's mood got visibly cloudy. "I ran a lot of elections...I neglected other things for them!" He looked ready to mist over. "I'm 75 years old!"

Laura winced. In the past she must have heard some variation of the age thing. But there was more here. He was old, but he was still Daddy. Stubborn. His girl may have married, but without his permission, it meant nothing. But it was only a game. He knew that his stubbornness meant nothing. Laura knew that it meant nothing. But it hurt nonetheless. It was between them, half-forgotten, still raw. It was everybody's second marriage—Joe's, Carolyn's, Laura's and mine— but in some alternative universe, none of that had happened.

When they got up to leave, I felt like I'd been in a wrestling match. All my muscles hurt. At the door Carolyn launched into another story. I shook Joe's hand. Laura lingered with Carolyn while I retreated into the room and started playing chess with myself.

Laura looked as if she'd trekked through a swamp.

"That man." She shook her head. "Carolyn told me why they were in town."

"Why? To wish you well in your marriage? Which they haven't mentioned?"

She shook her head. "He's getting operated on. A tumor in his neck."

I shook my head, too. Can't win, one way or another. If the opinions don't get you, life will. Diversity. What a joke.

Andrei Codrescu *immigrated to the United States in 1966 from Romania, where he was born in 1946. He is a poet, novelist, essayist, screenwriter and columnist for national and international publications, and his memoir, "The Hole in the Flag: A Romanian Exile's Story of Return and Revolution," was a Notable Book in 1991 and 1992. He is a regular contributor to National Public Radio, MSNBC, "Nightline," the New York Times, the Boston Globe, the Philadelphia Inquirer, the Chicago Tribune, Newsday and Playboy and is the MacCurdy Distinguished Professor of English at Louisiana State University in Baton Rouge, where he also edits the online literary journal Exquisite Corpse. His latest book, a historical novel, is "Casanova in Bohemia."*

A Measure of Acceptance

Floyd Skloot

The psychiatrist's office was in a run-down industrial section at the northern edge of Oregon's capital, Salem. It shared space with a chiropractic health center, separated from it by a temporary divider that wobbled in the current created by opening the door. When I arrived a man sitting with his gaze trained on the spot I suddenly filled began kneading his left knee, his suit pants hopelessly wrinkled in that one spot. Another man, standing beside the door and dressed in overalls, studied the empty wall and muttered as he slowly rose on his toes and sank back on his heels. Like me, neither seemed happy to be visiting Dr. Peter Avilov.

Dr. Avilov specialized in the psychodiagnostic examination of disability claimants for the Social Security Administration. He made a career of weeding out hypochondriacs, malingerers, fakers, people who were ill without organic causes. There may be many such scam artists working the disability angle, but there are also many legitimate claimants. Avilov worked as a kind of hired gun, paid by an agency whose financial interests were best served when he determined that claimants were not disabled. It was like having your house appraised by the father-in-law of your prospective buyer, like being stopped by a traffic cop several tickets shy of his monthly quota, like facing a part-time judge who works for the construction company you're suing. Avilov's incentives were not encouraging to me.

I understood why I was there. After a virus I contracted in December of 1988 targeted my brain, I became totally disabled. When the Social Security Administration decided to re-evaluate my medical condition eight years later, they exercised their right to send me to a doctor of their own choosing. This seemed fair enough. But after receiving records, test results and reports of brain scans and statements from my own internal-medicine and infectious-diseases physicians, all attesting to my ongoing disability, and after requiring 25 pages of handwritten questionnaires from me and my wife, they scheduled an appointment for me with Avilov. Not with an independent internal-medicine or infectious-diseases specialist, not with a neurologist, but with a shrink.

Now, 12 years after first getting sick, I've become adept at being brain-damaged. It's not that my symptoms have gone away; I still try to dice a stalk of celery with a carrot instead of a knife, still reverse "p" and "b" when I write, or draw a primitive hourglass when I mean to draw a star. I call our *bird feeder* a *bread winner* and place newly purchased packages of frozen corn in the dishwasher instead of the freezer. I put crumpled newspaper and dry pine into our wood stove, strike a match, and attempt to light the metal door. Preparing to cross the "main street" in Carlton, Ore., I look both ways, see a pickup truck a quarter-mile south, take one step off the curb, and land flat on my face, cane pointing due east.

So I'm still much as I was in December of 1988, when I first got sick. I spent most of a year confined to bed. I couldn't write and had trouble reading anything more complicated than People magazine or the newspaper's sports page. The functioning of memory was shattered, bits of the past clumped like a partly assembled jigsaw puzzle, the present a flicker of discontinuous images. Without memory it was impossible for me to learn how to operate the new music system that was meant to help me pass the time, or figure out why I felt so confused, or take my medications without support.

But in time I learned to manage my encounters with the world in new ways. I shed what no longer fit my life: training shoes and road-racing flats, three-piece suits and ties, a car. I bought a cane. I seeded my home with pads and pens so that I could write reminders before forgetting what I'd thought. I festooned my room with color-coded Post-it Notes telling me what to do, whom to call, where to locate important items. I remarried, finding love when I imagined it no longer possible. Eventually I moved to the country, slowing my external life to match its internal pace, simplifying, stripping away layers of distraction and demands.

Expecting the unexpected now, I can, like an improvisational actor, incorporate it into my performance. For instance my tendency to use words that are close to—but not exactly—the words I'm trying to say has led to some surprising discoveries in the composition of sentences. A freshness emerges when the mind is unshackled from its habitual ways. I never would have described the effect of a viral attack on my brain as being "geezered" overnight if I hadn't first confused the words *seizure* and *geezer*. It is as though my word-finding capacity has developed an associative function to compensate for its failures of precision, so I end up with *shellac* instead of *plaque* when trying to describe the gunk on my teeth. Who knows, maybe James Joyce was brain-damaged when he wrote "Finnegan's Wake," built a whole novel on puns and neologisms that were actually symptoms of disease.

It's possible to see such domination of the unexpected in a positive light. So getting lost in the familiar woods around our house and finding my way home again adds a twist of excitement to days that might seem circumscribed or routine because of my disability. When the natural-food grocery where we shop rearranged its entire stock, I was one of the few customers who didn't mind, since I could never remember where things were anyway. I am less hurried and more deliberate than I was; being attentive, purposeful in movement, lends my life an intensity of awareness that was not always present before. My senses are heightened, their fine-tuning mechanism busted. Spicy food, stargazer lilies in bloom, birdsong, heat, my wife's vivid palette when she paints—all have become more intense and stimulating. Because it threatens my balance, a sudden breeze is something to stop for, to let its strength and motion register. That may not guarantee success—as my pratfall in Carlton indicates—but it does allow me to appreciate detail and nuance.

One way of spinning this is to say that my daily experience is often spontaneous and exciting. Not fragmented and intimidating, but unpredictable, continuously new. I may lose track of things, or of myself in space, my line of thought, but instead of getting frustrated, I try to see this as the perfect time to stop and figure out what I want or where I am. I accept my role in the harlequinade. It's not so much a matter of making lemonade out of life's lemons but rather of learning to savor the shock, taste, texture and aftereffects of a mouthful of unadulterated citrus.

Acceptance is a deceptive word. It suggests compliance, a consenting to my condition and to who I have become. This form of acceptance is often seen as weakness, submission. We say *I accept my punishment.* Or *I accept your decision.* But such assent, while passive in essence, does provide the stable, rocklike foundation for coping with a condition that will not go away. It is a powerful passivity, the Zen of Illness, that allows for endurance.

There is, however, more than endurance at stake. A year in bed, another year spent primarily in my recliner—these were times when endurance was the main issue. But over time I began to recognize the possibilities for transformation. I saw another kind of acceptance as being viable, the kind espoused by Robert Frost when he said, "Take what is given, and make it over your own way." That is, after all, the root meaning of the verb "to accept," which comes from the Latin *accipere,* or "to take to oneself." It implies an embrace. Not a giving up but a welcoming. People encourage the sick to resist, to fight back; we say that our resistance is down when we contract a virus. But it wasn't possible to resist the effects of brain damage. Fighting to speak rapidly and clearly, as I always had in the past, only leads to more garbling of meaning; willing myself to walk without a cane or climb a ladder only leads to more falls; demanding that I not forget something only makes me angrier when all I can remember is the effort not to forget. I began to realize that the most aggressive act I could perform on my own behalf was to stop struggling and discover what I really could do.

This, I believe, is what the Austrian psychotherapist Viktor E. Frankl refers to in his classic book, "The Doctor and the Soul," as "spiritual elasticity." He says, speaking of his severely damaged patients, "Man must cultivate the flexibility to swing over to another value-group if that group and that alone offers the possibility of actualizing values." Man must, Frankl believes, "temper his efforts to the chances that are offered."

Such shifts of value, made possible by active acceptance of life as it is, can only be achieved alone. Doctors, therapists, rehabilitation professionals, family members, friends, lovers cannot reconcile a person to the changes wrought by illness or injury, though they can ease the way. Acceptance is a private act, achieved gradually and with little outward evidence. It also seems never to be complete; I still get furious with myself for forgetting what I'm trying to tell my daughter during a phone call, humiliated when I blithely walk away with another shopper's cart of groceries or fall in someone's path while examining the lower shelves at Powell's Bookstore.

But for all its private essence, acceptance cannot be expressed purely in private terms. My experience did not happen to me alone; family, colleagues and friends, acquaintances all were involved. I had a new relationship with my employer and its insurance company, with federal and state government, with people who read my work. There is a social dimension to the experience of illness and to its acceptance, a kind of reciprocity between self and world that goes beyond the enactment of laws governing handicapped access to buildings or rules prohibiting discrimination in the workplace. It is in this social dimension that, for all my private adjustment, I remain a grave cripple and, apparently, a figure of contempt.

At least the parties involved agreed that what was wrong with me was all in my head. However, mine was disability arising from organic damage to the brain caused by a viral attack, not from psychiatric illness. The distinction matters; my disability status would not continue if my condition were psychiatric. It was in the best interests of the Social Security Administration for Dr. Avilov to say my symptoms were caused by the mind, were psychosomatic rather than organic in nature. And what was in their interests was also in Avilov's.

On high-tech scans, tiny holes in my brain make visually apparent what is clear enough to anyone who observes me in action over time: I no longer have "brains." A brain, yes, with many functions intact, but I'm not as smart or as quick or as steady as I was. Though I may not look sick, and I don't shake or froth or talk to myself, after a few minutes it becomes clear that something fundamental is wrong. My losses of cognitive capability have been fully measured and recorded. They were used by the Social Security Administration and the insurance company to establish my total disability, by various physicians to establish treatment and therapy programs, by a pharmaceutical company to establish my eligibility for participation in the clinical field trial of a drug that didn't work. I have a handicapped parking placard on the dashboard of my car; I can get a free return-trip token from the New York City subway system by flashing my Medicaid card. In this sense I have a public profile as someone who is disabled. I have met the requirements.

Further, as someone with quantifiable diminishment in IQ levels, impaired abstract reasoning and learning facility, scattered recall capacities and aptitudes that decrease as fatigue or distraction increases, I am of scientific use. When it serves their purposes, various institutions welcome me. Indeed they pursue me. I have been actively recruited for three experimental protocols run by Oregon Health Sciences University. One of these, a series of treatments using DMSO, made me smell so rancid that I turned heads just by walking into a room. But when it does not serve their purpose, these same institutions dismiss me. Or challenge me. No matter how well I may have adjusted to living with brain damage, the world I often deal with has not. When money or status is involved, I am positioned as a pariah.

So would Avilov find that my disability was continuing, or would he judge me as suffering from mental illness? Those who say that the distinction is bogus, or that the patient's fear of being labeled mentally ill is merely a cultural bias and ought not matter, are missing the point. Money is at stake; in our culture this means it matters very much. To all sides.

Avilov began by asking me to recount the history of my illness. He seemed as easily distracted as I was; while I stared at his checked flannel shirt, sweetly ragged mustache and the pen he occasionally put in his mouth like a pipe, Avilov looked from my face to his closed door to his empty notepad and back to my face, nodding. When I finished, he asked a series of diagnostic questions: Did I know what day it was (Hey, I'm here on the right day, aren't I?), could I name the presidents of the United States since Kennedy, could I count backward from 100 by sevens? During this series he interrupted me to provide a list of four unconnected words (such as *train argue barn vivid*), which I was instructed to remember for later recall. Then he asked me to explain what was meant by the expression "People who live in glass houses should not throw stones." I nodded, thought for a moment, knew that this sort of proverb relied on metaphor, which as a poet should be my great strength, and began to explain. Except that

I couldn't. I must have talked for five minutes, in tortuous circles, spewing gobbledygook about stones breaking glass and people having things to hide, shaking my head, backtracking as I tried to elaborate. But it was beyond me, as all abstract thinking is beyond me, and I soon drifted into stunned silence. Crashing into your limitations this way hurts; I remembered as a long-distance runner hitting the fabled "wall" at about mile 22 of the Chicago Marathon, my body depleted of all energy resources, feeding on its own muscle and fat for every additional step, and I recognized this as being a similar sensation.

For the first time, I saw something clear in Avilov's eyes. He saw me. He recognized this as real, the blathering of a brain-damaged man who still thinks he can think.

It was at this moment that he asked, "Why are you here?"

I nearly burst into tears, knowing that he meant I seemed to be suffering from organic rather than mental illness. Music to my ears. "I have the same question."

The rest of our interview left little impression. But when the time came for me to leave, I stood to shake his hand and realized that Avilov had forgotten to ask me if I remembered the four words I had by then forgotten. I did remember having to remember them, though. Would it be best to walk out of the room, or should I remind him that he forgot to have me repeat the words I could no longer remember? Or had I forgotten that he did ask me, lost as I was in the fog of other failures? Should I say *I can't remember if you asked me to repeat those words, but there's no need because I can't remember them?*

None of that mattered because Avilov, bless his heart, had found that my disability status remained as it was. Such recommendations arrive as mixed blessings; I would much rather not be as I am, but since I am, I must depend on receiving the legitimate support I paid for when healthy and am entitled to now.

There was little time to feel relieved because I soon faced an altogether different challenge, this time from the company that handled my disability-insurance payments. I was ordered to undergo a two-day "Functional Capacity Evaluation" administered by a rehabilitation firm they hired in Portland. A later phone call informed me to prepare for six and a half hours of physical challenges the first day and three hours more the following day. I would be made to lift weights, carry heavy boxes, push and pull loaded crates, climb stairs, perform various feats of balance and dexterity, complete puzzles, answer a barrage of questions. But I would have an hour for lunch.

Wear loose clothes. Arrive early.

With the letter had come a warning: "You must provide your best effort so that the reported measurements of your functional ability are valid." Again the message seemed clear: *No shenanigans, you! We're wise to your kind.*

I think the contempt that underlies these confrontations is apparent. The patient, or—in the lingo of insurance operations—the claimant, is approached not only as an adversary but as a deceiver. *You can climb more stairs than that! You really can stand on one leg like a heron! Stop falling over, freeloader! We know that game.* Paranoia rules; here an institution seems caught in its grip. With money at stake, the disabled are automatically supposed to be up to some kind of chicanery, and our displays of symptoms are viewed as untrustworthy. Never mind that I contributed to Social Security for my entire working life, with the mutual understanding that if I were disabled, the fund would be there for me. Never mind that both my employer and I paid for disability insurance, with the mutual understanding that if I were disabled, payments would be there for me. Our doctors are suspect, our caregivers implicated. *We've got our eyes on you!*

The rehab center looked like a combination gym and children's playground. The staff were friendly, casual. Several were administering physical therapy so that the huge room into which I was led smelled of sweat. An elderly man at a desk worked with a small stack of blocks. Above the blather of Muzak, I heard grunts and moans of pained effort: a woman lying on mats, being helped to bend damaged knees; a stiff-backed man laboring through his stretches; two women side by side on benches, deep in conversation as they curled small weights.

The man assigned to conduct my Functional Capacity Evaluation looked enough like me to be a cousin. Short, bearded, thick hair curling away from a lacy bald spot, Reggie shook my hand and tried to set me at ease. He was good at what he did, lowering the level of confrontation, expressing compassion, concerned about the effect on my health of such strenuous testing. I should let him know if I needed to stop.

Right then, before the action began, I had a moment of grave doubt. I could remain suspicious, paranoia begetting paranoia, or I could trust Reggie to be honest, to assess my capacities without prejudice. The presence of patients being helped all around me seemed a good sign. This firm didn't appear dependent upon referrals for evaluation from insurance companies; they had a lucrative operation independent of that. And if I could not trust a man who reminded me of a healthier version of myself, it seemed like bad karma. I loved games and physical challenges. But I knew who and what I was now; it would be fine if I simply let him know as well. Though much of my disability results from cognitive deficits, there are physical manifestations, too, so letting Reggie know me in the context of a gym-like setting felt comfortable. Besides, he was sharp enough to recognize suspicion in my eyes, which would give him reason to doubt my efforts. We were both after the same thing: a valid representation of my abilities. Now was the time to put all I had learned about acceptance on the line. It would require a measure of acceptance on both sides.

What I was not prepared for was how badly I would perform in every test. I knew my limitations but had never measured them. Over a dozen years, the consequences of exceeding my physical capabilities had been made clear enough that I learned to live within the limits. Here I was brought repeatedly to those limits and beyond. After an hour with Reggie, I was ready to sleep for the entire next month. The experience was crushing. How could I comfortably manage only 25 pounds in the floor-to-waist lift repetitions? I used to press 150 pounds as part of my regular weekly training for competitive racing. How could I not stand on my left foot for more than two seconds? You shoulda seen me on a ball field! I could hold my arms up for no more than 75 seconds, could push a cart loaded with no more than 40 pounds of weights, could climb only 66 stairs. I could not fit shapes into their proper holes in a form-board in the time allotted, though I distinctly remember playing a game with my son that worked on the same principles and always beating the timer. Just before lunch Reggie asked me to squat and lift a box filled with paper. He stood behind me and was there as I fell back into his arms.

As Dr. Avilov had already attested, I was not clinically depressed, but this evaluation was almost enough to knock me into the deepest despair. Reggie said little to reveal his opinions. At the time, I thought that meant that he was simply being professional, masking judgment, and though I sensed empathy, I realized that that could be a matter of projection on my part.

Later I believed that his silence came from knowing what he had still to make me do. After lunch and an interview about the Activities of Daily Living form I had filled out, Reggie led me to a field of blue mats spread across the room's center. For a moment I wondered if he planned to challenge me to a wrestling match. That thought had lovely, symbolic overtones: wrestling with someone who suggested my former self; wrestling with an agent of *them*, a man certain to defeat me; or having my Genesis experience, like Jacob at Peniel wrestling with Him. Which, at least for Jacob, resulted in a blessing and a nice payout.

But no. Reggie told me to crawl.

In order to obtain "a valid representation" of my abilities, it was necessary for the insurance company to see how far and for how long and with what result I could crawl. It was a test I had not imagined, a test that could, in all honesty, have only one purpose. My ability to crawl could not logically be used as a valid measure of my employability. And in light of all the other tasks I had been unable to perform, crawling was not necessary as a measure of my functional limits. It would test nothing, at least nothing specific to my case, not even the lower limits of my capacity. Carrying the malign odor of indifference, tyranny's tainted breath, the demand that I crawl was almost comical in its obviousness: the paternal powers turning someone like me, a disabled man living in dependence upon their finances, into an infant.

I considered refusing to comply. Though the implied threat (*You must provide your best effort…*) contained in their letter crossed my mind, and I wondered how Beverly and I would manage without my disability payments, it wasn't practicality that made me proceed. At least I don't think so. It was, instead, acceptance. I had spent the morning in a public confrontation with the fullness of my loss, as though on stage with Reggie, representing the insurance company, as my audience. Now I would confront the sheer heartlessness of The System, the powers that demanded that I crawl before they agreed temporarily to accept my disability. I would, perhaps for the first time, join the company of those far more damaged than I am, who have endured far more indignity in their quest for acceptance. Whatever it was that

Reggie and the insurance company believed they were measuring as I got down on my hands and knees and began a slow circuit of the mats in the center of that huge room, I believed I was measuring how far we still had to go for acceptance.

Reggie stood in the center of the mats, rotating in place as I crawled along one side, turned at the corner, crossed to the opposite side, and began to return toward the point where I had started. Before I reached it, Reggie told me to stop. He had seen enough. I was slow and unsteady at the turns, but I could crawl fine.

I never received a follow-up letter from the insurance company. I was never formally informed of their findings, though my disability payments have continued.

At the end of the second day of testing, Reggie told me how I'd done. In many of the tests, my results were in the lower 5–10 percent for men my age. My performance diminished alarmingly on the second day, and he hadn't ever tested anyone who did as poorly on the dexterity components. He believed that I had given my best efforts and would report accordingly. But he would not give me any formal results. I was to contact my physician, who would receive Reggie's report in due time.

When the battery of tests had first been scheduled, I'd made an appointment to see my doctor a few days after their completion. I knew the physical challenges would worsen my symptoms and wanted him to see the result. I knew I would need his help. By the time I got there, he too had spoken to Reggie and knew about my performance. But my doctor never got an official report, either.

This was familiar ground. Did I wish to request a report? I was continuing to receive my legitimate payments; did I really want to contact my insurance company and demand to see the findings of my Functional Capacity Evaluation? Risk waking the sleeping dragon? What would be the point? I anticipated no satisfaction in reading that I was in fact disabled or in seeing how my experience translated into numbers or bureaucratic prose.

It seems that I was only of interest when there was an occasion to rule me ineligible for benefits. Found again to be disabled, I wasn't even due the courtesy of a reply. The checks came; what more did I need to show that my claims were accepted?

There was no need for a report. Through the experience, I had discovered something more vital than the measures of my physical capacity. The measure of public acceptance that I hoped to find, that I imagined would balance my private acceptance, was not going to come from a public agency or public corporation. It didn't work that way, after all. The public was largely indifferent, as most people, healthy or not, understand. The only measure of acceptance would come from how I conducted myself in public, moment by moment. With laws in place to permit handicapped access to public spaces, prevent discrimination, and encourage involvement in public life, there is general acceptance that the handicapped live among us and must be accommodated. But that doesn't mean they're not resented, feared, or mistrusted by the healthy. The Disability Racket!

I had encountered the true, hard heart of the matter. My life in the social dimension of illness is governed by forces that are severe and implacable. Though activism has helped protect the handicapped over the last four decades, there is little room for reciprocity between the handicapped person and his or her world. It is naive to expect otherwise.

I would like to think that the insurance company didn't send an official letter of findings because they were abashed at what they'd put me through. I would like to think that Dr. Avilov, who no longer practices in Salem, didn't move away because he found too many claimants disabled and lost his contract with the Social Security Administration. That my experience educated Reggie and his firm and that his report educated the insurance company, so everyone now understands the experience of disability or of living with brain damage.

But I know better. My desire for reciprocity between self and world must find its form in writing about my experience. Slowly. This essay has taken me 11 months to complete, in sittings of 15 minutes or so. Built of fragments shaped after the pieces were examined, its errors of spelling and of word choice and logic ferreted out with the help of my wife or daughter or computer's spell-checker. It may look to a reader like the product of someone a lot less damaged than I claim to be. But it's not. It's the product of someone who has learned how to live with his limitations and work with them. And when it's published, if someone employed by my insurance company reads it, I will probably get a letter in the mail demanding that I report for another battery of tests. After all, this is not how a brain-damaged man is supposed to behave.

Floyd Skloot's second book of essays, "In the Shadow of Memory," will appear in the spring of 2003 from the University of Nebraska Press. His essays were included in "The Best American Essays 2000," "The Best Science Writing 2000" and "The Art of the Essay 1999." Skloot is also a poet and novelist, and his collection, "The Evening Light," won the 2001 Oregon Book Award in Poetry.

Gone in Translation

Kate Small

The house strains against too many occupants and a hot, hard wind. A white man of 40 with no socks but shoes, next to him a white woman with dark streaks on her apron and flour on her arms. A white boy with bandages and a stick. A white girl whose knees are black with grime—I have her neck. The picture is captioned by number and location. The chapter's theme is not "family" or "white" but the sucked landscape of the 1934 Dust Bowl. All face the camera but two chalky babies, who taste the dirt as though they know the dust unrolling around them is the point. The dog strains toward the surface. Drought careens over shack and carcass; dust wends in sleek, arid ditches past every vanishing point.

I close the book. Ketti is coming. I am a technical writer, and I teach people to read. I am a volunteer, a low-level attendant in the marriage of literacy to welfare. Ketti is my student. She is black. I am white. We are both about 30, and we are both dyslexic. For two years we have been meeting twice a week at Shabilsky's, where for 40 years more, Paulina Prszybylski has been serving ice cream and sandwiches to old Jewish men.

Ben Medofsky is a daily customer. He shakes his head at what he sees out the window, checking it against what he remembers of South Portland, Ore., before the freeways.

"The Sixth Street synagogue—*there*," he says. "Gone." He looks at his watch. He is waiting for a young woman who calls herself G, who says she's a dancer and strike organizer, and who has arranged to interview him here. Ben helped make the CIO in '34, and the AFL. He was harassed because he was IWW. His wife was clubbed in their home by the police and became deaf.

"You want this spaghetti water?" Luis yells to Paulina from the kitchen. She uses it to starch her aprons.

"Toss it," she says. Her white restaurant shoes are permanently untied because her feet are permanently swollen. Paulina is 69 and the last of the original Prszybylskis, a family whose name was phonetically translated to *Shabilsky's* for the awning, menus and thick, oval platters. She sighs past a sign in the window: 21 Days Left. In less than a month, the restaurant will close forever. It is being annexed into the rest of the block for a franchise superstore.

"Connect the words to the picture," I say to Ketti. "O-t-t-e-r. Say, '*An* otter.'"

The illustration, like many in adult-literacy texts, looks smirky and uncomfortable. A penciled cross between a squirrel and a dachshund holds a sign in a clown-gloved paw. "*A* history! *An* hour! *An* apple!" Landlocked, deformed, the otter is supposed to be perky but squints in a surprisingly miserable way.

Ketti's brows press down in effort. She looks as if she's trying to suck the print through her pupils. "Don't say it before I try to read it," she reminds me gently. She memorizes everything she hears. She can't help it.

Ben's nurse, Janine, pushes through the glass door. She comes to find him here because he won't go to the clinic anymore. She asks for coffee at the counter.

"Order me a hot fudge," he yells to her, "no nuts."

"You got that right," Janine says.

"Another comedienne," Ben says. He has prostate cancer.

Janine takes a blood-pressure cuff out of her backpack. Ben's eyes go back to the TV mounted high in the corner behind the counter. It's always on.

"Circle the main verb and underline the subject," I say. "'Example: Beavers live in colonies, one or more family groups to a lodge. Example: A family usually consists of a mated pair and two sets of offspring.'"

Ketti pulls my library book across the table. It falls open to the picture. "That horseshoe," she says, "flaps at an *un*lucky angle."

"Maybe," I say.

Maybe I have an uncle in this photograph, one of 30,000 Depression-era Farm Securities documents. Maybe this is a picture of the hushed-over relative, the problem kin for whom genealogical nostalgia is forfeited.

The subject here is inheritance: what runs in the family, what is molecular and predisposed, carried in blood and bone, heritable like blood pressure, height, weight and learning disabilities. The subject is visible skin, invisible things beneath it and the weight of the things deeded to us from the outside because of our hue.

I have been looking at the farm picture because of a cousin, not a first or second one but removed, third or fourth. Last winter she sent out a laser-printed holiday letter with a snapshot of herself: 60-ish, flower-printed and hopeful on the steps of the Mormon genealogical library in Salt Lake City. She is hugging an accordion file. She has devoted herself to a history project inspired by the kind of family-tree software you can purchase at Wal-Mart and is hunting everyone down. Scrapbooks and rotten envelopes have been loosened from bi-coastal storage; unwanted bibles and packets of nameless photos have been jettisoned into the cousin's den in Iowa.

She thinks there is a "we" pictured in one of those famous Farm Securities photographs—gleaned from the nose in *this* photo, the hands in *that*, this child, that house, a horse, a forehead, a pair of boots. She says my last name, Small, is a translation of the Polish—originally *Maly*. The cousin describes the tabular kinship chart she's drawn, the branches and roots of which burrow back to the old country. She wants to do the whole thing in needlepoint.

Before I write back, I find the photo to which she refers in the library. It does look "familiar." But at least in part because you see these pictures so often in American history textbooks. They seem to say everything about sharecropping, famine and erosion. And lately they've had a new life selling things: insurance, pesticides, lawn chemicals, mortgages. "Wish *I'd* had a Beauty Mist Humidifier!" a balloon over a desiccated farmwoman is likely to say.

We must be at enough distance from the severity of the original moment that the picture may rehydrate itself, shuck its early, craggier meanings and go back to work as a cartoon, the way Janis Joplin's disembodied voice has been summoned from the grave to sell cars for Mercedes Benz.

Am I related to these people by blood, by culture, or both?

I haven't before now been interested in genealogy, but my cousin's letter makes me think of a conversation I heard between my grandmother and her sisters when I was eye-level with people's elbows.

"Now Josip Maly—he was *Klan*," I heard my grandmother whisper. I didn't know what *Klan* meant, but I knew it was something very bad. My grandmother was a weaver, and I was sitting under her huge floor loom, looking up through an acre of thread. I connected the K in *Klan* with the front end of my own name and a terrible possibility. What if the T sound at the end of Kate was the only thing that kept bad things from flowing out of me and poisoning other people? *Klan*: The word shuddered in my mouth and pinched my tongue with the stone lips of *clam*. My negligible last name, Small, became damp and heavy with shame by association, like a drowning kitten tied to a brick. Ever since, when I am in the vicinity of the word *Klan*, I always see—I am seeing it now—my head pushed through the tight warp of my grandmother's loom, my throat pressed upon by stiff, wool cord. I never said any of this to anybody. The whispering meant it was something you didn't talk about.

"Why did your people start out in Mississippi?" Ketti asks me at Shabilsky's.

"They saw Kosciusko on the map and thought they'd find a little Warsaw there. They were wrong. The town was named for an army general who directed the construction of West Point, who was granted estates, a pension and the rank of brigadier."

"My mother was born in Kosciusko," Ketti says. "So was my grandmother."

I smile at this thing in common because I have assumed for us some other ones: dyslexia, for one; our names, for another.

"You're a Katherine, right?" I ask.

"No, *you're* a Katherine," Ketti says.

"Then what are you?"

"Kenyatta." She spells it. Slowly, so that I'll learn it.

"Hey," Ben says. "Oprah Winfrey is from Kosciusko, too, you know." He's right. Ben watches a lot of "Oprah."

"Underline the subject," I say. "'Musk glands in both sexes produce a liquid used in perfumes.'" We keep reading about beavers. We order

Cokes. I am supposed to help Ketti prepare for a class in which the students will pretend to operate a restaurant. We are supposed to write a resumé, role-play a job interview, practice being waitresses and bus boys. We are supposed to finish our workbook in two weeks.

Ben is parked at his corner table. Paulina and Ben have a 20-year-old hostility pact. When Paulina is in the kitchen, Ben calls her a Nazi collaborator behind her back because her family survived in Krakow during the war, a stone's throw from Auschwitz.

"They knew and they did nothing," Ben mutters.

Paulina's parents had a small village farm in Poland. They died during the war, and their children sold milk to soldiers. Those children came here in steerage. They landed in Nova Scotia, crossed Canada and went south.

But Paulina doesn't like Ben because he comes every day but he never leaves a tip.

The dancer who didn't show up a few days ago does and introduces herself as G. Her head is shaved, and her eyes are sharp and dark. She walks fast and weighs about 90 pounds.

"What kind of dancer are you, anyway?" Ben says.

"Exotic," G says.

"A stripper? Ben asks, "Where?"

"Two blocks from here."

"There goes the neighborhood," Ben says. He waves her away. She waits a few minutes at the counter, then leaves. Ben and Luis, the dishwasher, don't like each other, but they talk about G as soon as she's gone.

"I guess that's why they call Oregon the Beaver State," Luis says.

"Shut up," Janine says.

"Well, I just don't see how a bunch of skinny girls in fishnets is going to union up," Ben says, "and *Underplush*—what kind of name is that for a decent establishment?"

Ketti, Ben, Paulina, Luis, G, Janine and I live in Portland, Ore., a town sliced by rivers and freeways, a moist, mossy place still surprised by unemployment and housing shortages but ready to insist that welfare recipients prove they are engaged in activities that increase their employability. For 10 years Ketti has cleaned houses in Lake Oswego, a suburb of Portland three buses away from where she lives. But in the last two years, she has developed a pain in her spine that won't go away. She has been to doctors but has no health insurance and, having ruled out anything life threatening, doesn't seek other treatment. She can't bend over.

"What does it feel like?" I ask.

"The ache is dark blue," she says. "The ache is shaped like a figure 8."

Ketti and I have access to extra color. I see pink after I eat spinach. Ketti says milk has a rust-colored taste and the silky weight of mercury. I taste sounds; she hears shapes. When we compare these kinds of notes, we whisper.

I give Ketti a worksheet and go back to my picture. Like many dyslexics Ketti and I take a great deal from images—we are translators at the same time that we doubt a picture's surface candor. Today something floats up from the farm photograph, from beneath the stumps, milkweed and broken rakes, lurking in the kicked jars and snapped wheels: a stench, pulsing through the sockets in the wall, in the steam rising from laundry, congealing around an unseen hood.

"You're making me seasick," Ben says from his table. I am rocking a little.

Paulina changes the number in the window.

For five days the stripper tries to get Ben to talk to her, but he won't.

Ben tries to get his coffee warmed up, but Paulina ignores him.

Paulina's Chevy Citation gets towed from the alley where she has parked for six years.

Ketti and I alternate the literacy workbook with the Oregon DMV handbook because Ketti has to prove she's taken a driver's test, even if she fails. I point to a picture of cars A, B and C poised between arrows, driving urgently around the curves of a suburban rotary. "Who has the right of way?" I ask.

"Looks like a cold front coming in," Ketti says.

Paulina changes the number in the window.

When the sign says 12 Days Left, the stripper comes in again. She's wearing a T-shirt that says "Bad Girls Like Good Contracts."

"My two cents?" Ben says as soon as she comes in the door. "You want to organize, do it. But don't count on anything. That ship sailed. They won't treat you like a heroine. And a bunch of strippers— excuse me, *exotic dancers*—people won't give you the time of day."

"Why are you being such a jerk?" G says.

"Get a real job," Ben says to her. "And you— " he points at Ketti, "get any job."

Ketti smiles. "Well, that's an improvement," she says to me.

"How?" I say.

"He's talking *to* me."

Usually Ben waits for her to leave before he rants. Ben watched the first wave of African-Americans come to Portland to build ships for Kaiser in the '40s. He organized many of these people. But he saw a second massive black migration in the '60s, much more character- ized by un- and underemployment. Ben is a union man, but he still thinks of welfare as wasteful public assistance. He doesn't, however, think of Social Security as welfare. Nor does he view unemployment compensation or workers' compensation as welfare; he believes he is entitled to those benefits because he worked for them.

G leans over his table and gets in his face. "Who died and made you Rosa Parks?"

"Because of nice, ordinary people like me," Ben says, "there's a labor board and the Fair Labor Standards Act. We *made* Social Security in 1935."

"So how come I'm not good enough to organize?"

Ben stares at the rings in G's nose. He scowls. "Okay. Fine. Free speech is one of the foundations on which our democracy rests. But a little constructive criticism: Stop with the tattoos and the hardware all over. I know what I'm talking about. Now what you want is your collective bargaining."

Janine applauds.

G sits down to take notes.

Ketti orders a sandwich.

Paulina changes the number in the window.

The sign says Nine Days Left. We eat spaghetti and watch "Oprah." The show is about "emotional intelligence." Oprah's guest expert describes the outcome of a study begun 30 years earlier. We see video-tape of a researcher seated in a room with a 4½-year-old child.

The researcher places a marshmallow on a plate before the boy.

"You can eat that marshmallow right *now*," the researcher says. "But if you *wait* until I come back, then you can have *two* marshmallows. If you don't want to wait, you can eat the first marshmallow, but you *won't* get the second one." This exercise is repeated with other children.

The researcher follows these children for 20-plus years. Generally those who resisted the temptation to eat the first marshmallow have better grades, higher test scores and bigger incomes, and stay married.

Generally all of the divorced, unemployed, jailed, drug-addicted, alcoholic are in the group that grabbed the first marshmallow without waiting.

Nobody at Shabilsky's says anything. We all know that we would have eaten the first marshmallow.

"What if you're hungry?" Ketti finally says.

"What if you didn't have breakfast?" G says.

"What if you have a sweet tooth?" Paulina says. She's diabetic.

The children were preschoolers at the Stanford University School of Education daycare center.

"What about everybody else?" I ask.

"What a crock," Ben says.

Then the real-estate attorney for the franchise superstore comes in. He smiles with a lot of teeth.

"Soon you'll be able to get 63 flavors of ice cream here," he says to everybody.

"Who needs 63?" Ben says.

"I need about four," Janine says.

The lawyer orders a half-decaf cappuccino, dry.

"We don't have that," Paulina says.

The lawyer gives Paulina a check for $34,000. It's not nearly enough. But there are people who can't afford to delay gratification, who know that you don't turn down a sure thing in a world so slippery.

"I've seen that lawyer at the club," the exotic dancer says. She's sitting at a booth with a laptop and a huge glass of water.

Somehow the lawyer has sucked all the air out of Shabilsky's. Then Paulina reads it in our faces: All of a sudden we're all on the same side of something.

"There are other lawyers," I say, though I don't know any.

"We could make a petition," G says.

"Stand in front of the wrecking ball and all that," says Ketti.

"Kids," Paulina says, "I'm tired. I want to retire. What would we be saving?"

"*Shtetl*," Ben says. "That's what we'd be saving."

"You're right," she says, but her face says another thing, and we know it's over. All the other customers have long since stopped coming in.

"Nobody likes a countdown," Ben says.

"Nobody likes to watch something die," says Janine, the oncology nurse.

Two days later Ketti shows me an agency memorandum. I scan it for a reprieve, but it says public-assistance recipients must gain proficiency in standard English or become good readers in two years. It says public-assistance recipients will be fingerprinted. It says our time is up. We are on chapter three of our workbook.

"Say the forms of 'to be,'" I say: "be, am/are, being, was/were, been."

"She be busy," Ketti says, smiling. "There is more music in this grammar."

"Music is important," Janine says to us over the back of her booth. She pours hot butterscotch on a dish of pralines-and-cream.

"'Because it don't mean a thing,'" says G, "'without some fine *bada-bing*.'"

"*Swing*," Ben says. "It's *swing*."

"Like, duh," G says.

Ketti and Ben order grilled sandwiches, onion rings and peach ice cream. They are ordering as much food as they can so that Paulina will make a little money.

"Circle the main verb and underline the subject," I say. "'The beaver's coat, consisting of a dense, fine underfur, is tan to dark brown above, paler below.'"

"I'm tired of beavers," Ketti says. "I want to read about something closer to home."

Paulina replaces the ketchup bottle on Ben's table.

Ben leaves a tip.

Ketti goes to her caseworker and says she wants a copy of her file. She gets this and brings it to me.

"'Probably Fragile X,'" I read from the box marked *Assessment*.

Then Ketti goes to the library. She comes back with a book.

"'The syndrome is so named,'" I read from it, "'because a small area of the X-chromosome has a tendency to break.'"

We learn that X-linked disorders manifest more clearly in boys because boys have only one X-chromosome. Girls have two X-chromosomes, but even though the "good" one might override the "bad" one, one of the two X-chromosomes in every cell is inactive. In these females, the book says, Fragile X causes a language disorder called *cluttering*.

It's likely she has "congenital word blindness," Ketti's file says. And in addition to spelling characterized by order errors, left and mis-handedness, stammering, headaches and eye pain, she, like some other dyslexics, "seems to have defects of the sense organs."

The book says learning disabilities run in families. The child of an affected parent has a 50-50 chance of inheriting dyslexia.

"My parents don't have it," I say. "Do yours?"

"My mother reads. My grandmother didn't. I may assume my great-grandmother didn't, either, but that's different."

"How?" I ask.

Ketti smiles. "Baby, you're just a little bit slow, and I don't mean dyslexia. I mean slow like every other Marsha-damn-Brady in the U.S. of A."

"*Jan*," I say. "It was Jan. She was clumsy, and she had glasses."

"Yeah, well, boohoo," Ketti says.

Ketti means of course that her great-grandmother didn't read because she was a slave. And she's pointing out another thing: Nobody ever wrote *Fragile X* on my file. Nobody made a file for me at all.

In fact my disability was and is subtle, partly because my parents tended it at home with a lot of time and attention. It is impossible to overstress my good fortune there. When I ate peanuts and said "Green" —when I pointed left-handed to my father's radio and said it sounded like salad dressing—my parents told me that I had secret, infra-red seeing, infra-blue and infra-yellow. And so I have the *privilege*—and I choose that word for all of its class and race connotations—of finding it odd that anyone would call my dyslexia a "disability." My parents kept me innocent, a gift there is no repaying. But that innocence has kept me *ignorant*, and I choose *that* word, too, for its class and race connotations.

It is heresy to say from within the pedagogical arm of public policy that I wouldn't want *not* to have my dyslexia. I know that plenty of other people who have it would be better off without it, or at least with a milder form, like mine. But my dyslexia has facilitated a kind of exertion, without which I would feel lost, for making and looking at sentences. That tug and strain is as fundamental to me as gravity.

The training I got for tutoring dyslexics, while admittedly minimal, approached this condition as if it were a defect that needed to be excised or changed—like a harelip.

I would miss my dyslexia badly if it were gone. Text just isn't only text. The white spaces between words, between letters—even the seraphs on different fonts—*mean*. Printed language presents almost three-dimensionally. Sometimes everything in a word doubles—not just its letters, but its weight and intensity—as message. Sometimes when I am very tired, I feel bombarded. Letters are mosquitoes I want to fan away, but they are enclosed around my head within a bowl. They flash and strobe; they pile up like thousands of dead ants on the surfaces of my eyeballs. Yet when writing goes well for me, it feels as if I have painted dots on a balloon, and as I blow up the balloon, the dots, my words, expand away from each other, held but lifted by helium. It is such a fine pleasure, with a little pain underneath, like the tingling under a scab as it begins to pull away from healing skin. An itch like carbonation.

I ask Ketti if she wants to write.

"Write? Sister, I want to *read*. I want to read and read and read."

"'Fragile X disorder is a common cause of mild mental retardation,'" G reads out loud. She stops.

"No, it's okay," Ketti says.

"'These children are often recognizable by their large heads, prominent ears and long, narrow jaws.'"

Everyone looks at Ketti and me.

"Jaws not very long," Ben says.

"Small heads, too," says Janine.

"Tiny ears," Paulina says to Ketti. "Not yours, honey," she says to me. "Yours are pretty big."

"So you're not retarded," Ben says.

"Thank you," Ketti says.

G taps the page. "You know what this is?" she says. "This is name-calling."

Ben shudders. Janine looks at him carefully.

"You know what it reminds me of?" Ben says. "It reminds me of what Hitler's propaganda people said. That was their kind of talk."

"Yes," Paulina says. "It sounded so confident."

Paulina and Ben sigh in tandem. They look old.

Four Days Left. Everyone orders marshmallow parfaits. Ketti and I throw out the workbook.

"*Bialy jak kreda*," Paulina says in Polish.

"White as a sheet," Ben translates.

"Do you speak Polish?" I ask Ben.

"Does the pope?" he says.

"*Stary jak swiat*," Ben says.

"Old as the hills," Paulina translates.

Ketti looks up from her library book. She and G are reading about synesthesia, which means "extra sense."

"It's a name for our sense-crossing," Ketti says to me.

I pick up the book. All babies have it, I read, but as the brain develops, multisensory connections go away—sense responses part ways. That is what's supposed to happen. In the brain of a normal person, information from single-sense zones flows one way into a multisensory zone. There are routes going back again, but for most of us, those roads back are blocked.

"Backward and forward," Ketti says to me.

I hear these words, and I feel a feathery brushing of gold in the small of my back.

"Bright," I say, and, "soft/heavy."

Ketti nods and smiles and holds my gaze. The TV commercial behind us tastes like mustard. Paulina's voice sounds pointed. The turkey sandwich on my plate is round-flavored. The page is shedding light up.

We have three days. I start writing my own captions for the farm photograph. I itemize things on unpictured shelves and what might be behind the house.

Paulina puts the Closed sign in the window, but we all stay until midnight.

In my notebook I refer to the unmentioned uncle as "you." My gaze fixes on the leathery boy away from the others. I heap upon him the future waiting in the gun and the torch and the rope coiled by the pump. I avoid the dog. I summon the outline of cloth, blank slices for eyes, a blood smell in its cotton warp. Grease and gasoline rise to the surface, crumbs and string, the pleas for mercy, the dog shot for barking.

G, Janine and Ben play canasta. Every time Ben gets a lousy hand, he takes a shot at G. "Appearance is important," he says, "and if you don't mind my asking, what's that thing in your face? Oy, your tongue too—you could be nice-looking."

You meet my eye but do not anticipate me, I write to the boy in the picture.

Light and dark lose their edges. Your shirt and ears have bleached themselves into the grass. After you are dead, a chemical firm will dump its mercury into your waters.

"How do you say *child*?" I ask Paulina.

"*Dziecko*," she says.

"What color is the word?" G asks.

"Silver," Ketti says.

Ben loses another game. "By the way," he says to G, "a little hair wouldn't hurt, if you don't mind my saying so. This bald thing you got going, it's like Dachau already. How is that good for business, is all I'm getting at."

On the morning of the last day, I get a postcard from my needle-pointing cousin.

"Guess what," she writes. "That photo I told you about? *It's not us.* Dang!"

Just like that, the document I have been gleaning for threads of proof is yanked out from under my own genealogical embroidery.

"Too bad," Ketti says. "You were getting attached to him."

"Yes," I say.

"Well, if it makes you feel any better, I'm sure somebody in his family did something bad to a Negro. Sorry there's no Rodney King video."

I probably look hurt.

"Honey, try to hold on to *all* the meanings of *'hood*. Nice *and* ugly."

"*Shtetl*," Paulina says.

Ben looks up. His eyes agree.

They're right. It's better to stay a little haunted. Anybody anywhere can become the tired, hungry Poles in Krakow, going about the hard business of living a stone's throw from mass murder. We're all so much closer to it than we know.

"And, anyway," Ketti sighs, "whoever he was, right there, at that moment, he's just a pale little boy."

G comes in and plunks a boom box on the counter. She pushes in a tape and dances. This scrawny girl with pencil legs in frayed jeans jigs her goodies to an Eastern European Klezmer band. She laughs and dances like a sapling, both weightless and rooted, like a tree in Colorado somewhere, with white bark and hard, shiny leaves. What mesmerizes us is the expression in her hands, their peculiar flexibility and long, tapered fingernails lacquered in opal.

We clap.

She shrugs and unplugs the machine.

This is when we find out Ketti is a song database—a walking jukebox. She sings "Wild Thing," "Tiny Bubbles" and "Fly Me to the Moon." She knows all the words to all the verses—she can't help it. Her face is as incandescent as chords from a church organ. When she sings "Moon River," Ben stands up, and with a pristine, aged formality, he takes Paulina's hand.

They wend very slowly through a waltz learned in childhood. It is heartbreakingly lovely.

Ben sits down heavily and buys G a strawberry malt. "Quit this, already," he says to her, "what you're doing at that place." He's talking about her job.

"You never looked at dirty pictures?" She says. She turns around and stares him down.

"Oy," Ben says. "You could call this 'sitting shiva,'" he says, "or you could call it watching a train wreck."

The restaurant is closed, and Paulina is selling everything at Shabilsky's. She's going to Palm Springs for a few weeks, then getting some dental work done.

G buys the boat-shaped sundae dishes. Ben buys the long-handled spoons. Ketti buys coffee mugs. Janine buys the neon sign. I buy a Formica-topped table with a boomerang pattern.

Thank You for 44 Years, a sign says in the window.

Luis pulls a burn can to the alley and loads it with paper, gas and a broken chair.

Ben hands everybody a skewer and breaks out a bag of marshmallows. "Eat as many as you want," he says. "I got three bags."

Paulina holds up her palms and considers the long lives of her hands, pinked up over the flame.

"I don't even like marshmallow," Ben says.

"Me, neither," G says.

"Can't stand them," Paulina says.

"What is marshmallow made of, anyway?" I ask.

"You don't want to know," Janine says.

"Give me s'more," Ketti says.

Luis drops his apron in the burn can. The smell of charred sugar is beautiful and curls around us. The marshmallows turn black and spark.

"Now *this* is *shtetl*," Ben says.

"What's *shtetl*?" Ketti asks.

"It's not the same thing as neighborhood," Ben says.

"It's *this*," Paulina says.

"It's green," I say.

"Nope," Kenyatta says, with sugar in her mouth. "It's a whole lot of aqua-blue."

Kate Small's work has appeared in Nimrod, Boston Review, Madison Review, Chelsea, Other Voices and "Best New American Voices," a Harcourt anthology edited by Tobias Wolff. She is the recipient of the Lorian Hemingway Prize, the Vogelstein Foundation Grant and National Endowment for the Arts fellowship. She resides in Portland, Ore.

Mixed-Blood Stew

Jewell Parker Rhodes

*I*t was an old document. Rough parchment, yellowed and withered. I was all of 10, on the threshold of womanhood, digging in my mother's closet, trying to find clues about why my mother abandoned me when I was an infant, why she returned to claim me when I was 9. On this sweltering, summer day, I found a treasure trove of documents—birth certificates, Social Security cards with various names, paycheck stubs and blurred photographs of my mother with strangers. But I knew I'd discovered something special when I uncovered the fragile sheet sandwiched between cardboard and tissue paper.

> *SLAVE AUCTION*
> *Various goods and animals to be auctioned,*
> *including one healthy male, a woman (good cook), and child.*
> *Wright Plantation*
> *Respectable offers only*

"What are you doing?"

My hands trembled, but rather than retreating, I asked, "What this?"

"I don't like you going through my things." She took the package from my hand and laid it on the bed.

"That your family?" I asked. Of course they were my family, too. But Mother had been gone so long I couldn't help thinking of her as separate from me.

Almost whispering, Mother traced the dulled letters with her fingers. "The good cook. She was my great-grandmother. The man, her husband. The child, my grandmother. Master Wright sold them like cattle. When slavery ended, my folks claimed Master's name because they were his kin."

Kin, I knew, was a code word for rape. Race-mixing. Miscegenation. The child was mulatto. The "healthy male" who raised her wasn't her father. Nonetheless, the small family, lucky to be sold together, took Wright's name and created another, darker limb of his family tree.

For a brief moment, I thought Mother would slap me. Or ground me. Or scream, making me cower, cover my ears.

"This is mine," she said and layered the auction sheet beneath tissue paper and taped the cardboard shut.

But I knew she was wrong—it was mine, too—part of my blood. I reached out to give her a hug, but Mother pulled away.

"Don't touch my things again."

After Mother left I had a vision of a handsome black man and woman riding on a wagon perch with a yellow-brown girl between them. When the child's hand clasped a parent's, did she ever wonder about her lighter skin? About the faces stirring inside her blood?

Mother had the auction sheet framed but never hung it. Until her death it remained shelved in a closet—a buried reminder of what my mother considered a secret. What was worth hiding from neighbors' and her children's eyes. Wipe away roots. Mother created herself full-blown, sprung from the head of Zeus. Mother was all charm, respectability; in her mind her people arrived on the Mayflower, never anchored belowdecks in a slave-ship's hold.

I'd always known mysterious people were stirring in my blood.

During the nine years of my mother's absence, my paternal grandmother raised me. Raised me in the A.M.E. Methodist Church and in a community with its own special rainbow. Red-toned Miss Chalmers, sandy-faced Willie, black-beyond-midnight Reverend, and ivory-skinned Mrs. Jackson. Dozens of words described our myriad colors: *Chocolate. Coffee. Café au lait. High yellow. Indigo. Bronze.* Street-corner boys whistled at the parade of sepia girls. Proud church women declared our deacons "fine, righteous black men." And on Easter Sundays, with pastels adorning black and brown bodies, I knew each and every one of us was beautiful.

"African-American people, like all people, be rich within themselves," my grandmother said. We grandkids—my sister, Tonie, my cousin Aleta and I—sitting on porch steps, sucking on salted ice or feeding grass to lightning bugs trapped inside a jar, would listen as Grandmother, her voice rising and falling like a sermon, told us tales of ourselves.

"We come from Georgia. Before that—Africa. White folks didn't understand there be thousands of tribes. Each with its own history. Slavers thought anybody with black skin be ignorant, be blank slates for them to write upon and breed. Foolishness."

"Hun-hunh," we testified, drawing people with white chalk, printing our names in block letters. If it was especially hot and humid, we'd pretend we were in church and fan ourselves with newspapers folded like accordions.

"Once black folks could fly. They came from a special tribe with magic words. One day when Master worked them too hard, beat them too long, they played their bodies like drums. Foot-stomping. Hand-clapping. Chest- and thigh-beating. Sent the message, 'Tonight. We fly.'

"Come midnight, when day blends into the next, they strapped their babies on their backs, whispered their magic, and lifted off the ground like crows. Blackbirds in the sky. Sailing high across the fields and above the seas."

"How come we couldn't fly?" I asked.

"Somebody needed to tell the tale. Like I be telling you. Like one day you be telling your children."

Tonie giggled. "I ain't marrying."

I elbowed my sister, declaring, "I'll tell."

Tonie rolled her eyes, stuck out her tongue.

Grandmother laughed, patting my back, making me feel special.

"White folks used to say one drop of black blood makes you a slave. Made it a law, too. Sheer foolishness. Pepper in the pot makes everything taste better. Can't use just salt."

"You saying we a stew?"

"Yes. The best kind. Mixed-blood stew."

Then Grandmother, noticing the sky filled with twinkling stars and a crescent moon, shooed us to bed and dreams of clouds cradling us. Dreams of ancestors flying, filling a pot with laughter and love.

Grandmother's tales were better than my mother's silence. Cross-racial diversity didn't imply any shame, only grace.

One summer Grandmother blessed us with a vacation trip to Georgia. We grandkids frolicked, skipped across grass, marveling at homes made of wood rather than brick. Marveling at one-story houses with acres of pecan and orange trees. Our three-story home had an L-shaped yard of concrete and just enough dirt for a rose bush, which rarely bloomed.

Blood memories of that southern visit still stir me. I remember glimpsing my great-grandmother, half Seminole, half black, sitting in the middle of her bed, wearing a white flannel gown. She was so frail I thought her a ghost. So silent I thought her mute.

I stood in the doorway watching her brush, over and over again, her long strands of black silk. Hair so long she could sit on it. Hair so dark it gleamed like polished rock.

For three days I watched her with each setting sun. Finally I asked, "Why does she do it, Grandmother? What for?"

"She's afraid water will make her catch cold. So she brushes away the dirt. Stroke by stroke."

"Hmmm," I murmured, my eyes sparkling.

"Don't you think it," answered Grandmother, knowing I dreaded shampoos and the hot comb pressing my kinky hair flat.

Grandfather, not to be outdone by Grandmother's line, had his own stories to tell.

"Seminole be all right. But I got Choctaw and Irish in me."

Sunday afternoons he'd be in his familiar spot, sitting at the head of the dining-room table, smoking a pipe and sipping Iron City beer. He'd grab anyone who passed by and tell his ancestral stories.

"In the '20s, Irish come to the Pittsburgh steel mills. Stood the heat 'like niggers,' some say. I say they stood the heat like men who appreciated an extra dollar at the end of the day." Then he'd jab his pipe. "Negroes got 50 cents.

"My Irish grand-dad, nearly bald, freckled all over, fell in love with my grandmother, who had some white in her from a generation before. She had Choctaw, too. Warrior blood. My grandmother's mama already had several of Master's children. One year, to spite him, she got pregnant by an Indian. Master was fit to be tied."

"So what all that blood makes me?"

He laughed, his mouth wide like a neighing horse. "Someone smart. Someone with the best of the best."

"Oh," I exhaled while Grandfather slapped his leg, his laughter ending in a fit of coughing.

As decades passed, our ethnic group kept changing, shifting, melding into more beautiful and varied gumbos, mixed-blood stews. Each marriage, each baby born yielded new blood.

White Americans insisted our bloodlines were uncomplicated. "One drop of black blood" had historical resonance.

In contemporary terms "one drop" meant bigots and Klansmen, thick-headed policemen and ignorant folk could kick, beat, lynch, verbally abuse you, regardless. There was no measure for diversity.

It was always white versus black.

Even when whites confronted a technically Anglo/Irish/Choctaw/ Cherokee/African girl. A nigger was a nigger was a nigger...even when she, like me, was an assistant professor at the University of Maryland walking home from educating young minds, enjoying the sunshine and startled into fury at being called a nigger by the frat-house boys.

I always wanted to know the bloodlines of my tormentors. How white was their whiteness? What secrets lived in their veins? Did delving into generations yield Asian, Pacific Islander, Hispanic and African, too? And if we went back to the beginning, the early dawn of our species, wasn't Lucy their mother, too?

In 1954 I was born and Emmett Till, 12, was murdered for speaking slang ("Hey, Baby") to an adult white woman. His mother insisted his coffin be open so everybody could see the battering of her baby boy.

Till's death sparked the birth of the civil rights movement. African-Americans demanded justice. Unity was our strength. But like wily and gifted tricksters, proud marchers knew they embodied "the other," embodied, in each and every one of them, some drop, *one drop* of Anglo-American blood.

Even a child knows there is no pure color. Everything comes from a mix. And like artists African-Americans have always embraced the mix, even when some of our blood mirrored our tormentors.

Living in my grandmother's house, I often dreamed about the faces inside my blood. As a child, stepping onto the bathtub rim, leaning against the bathroom sink, I'd stare into the mirror, pinching my skin. Freckles sprinkled across my nose—Irish? Black, slightly slanted eyes—Seminole? Hair curled tight about my face—African? For hours

I tried to account for how each part of me revealed the light and dark shadows in my blood.

In school I learned about Dick and Jane (who came to America from nowhere) and read all the tales about white families, rural and urban, rich and poor, living happily ever after in white houses with white picket fences. Fences that kept children like me out. Literature, I had discovered, was only about white lives. I smiled, kept reading nevertheless, for I knew my own joy and happiness being a brown girl raised in my grandmother's and grandfather's house.

One afternoon after my eighth birthday, I passed the dining-room table. A newspaper cutting lay in the center of it.

"That's your father's daddy," said Grandmother, coming to stand behind me.

"That's Grandfather Thornton?"

"No. I was married before. This is your father's daddy."

"He's white."

"He's dead."

A sad-eyed man seemed to stare right through me. He was in a naval uniform, handsome, with a high forehead like mine and a squared-off chin like Daddy's. Name given: "Lieutenant J. Parker." Bold head-line: "Served valiantly in the war." Plain print: "Age 56, survived by his wife and four kids."

"My grandfather's white?"

"Or else so light he passed. It wasn't clear. One time he told me he was French Canadian. Another time he said he was colored. Another time, Southern white."

I exhaled, excited by the revelation.

Grandmother turned away from the photo but left it on the dining-room table. I could see her down the short hallway, opening our freezer and pulling out Grandfather's (should I still call him that?) white shirts, all balled up and half frozen. "They iron better this way," Grandmother always told me.

I watched her lumber down the hallway, then into the living room to set up her ironing station. She turned the TV to the after-noon movies. Both Grandmother and I liked to watch Bette Davis in "Jezebel," Bob Hope in "Going Down to Rio," and Lon Chaney in "Abbott and Costello Meet Frankenstein."

Steam hissing from the flatiron, I asked, "Why you stopped being married to him—the other man?"

"In a way I didn't. He left. Said a sailor couldn't be an officer unless he be white. So he chose white."

"He passed?"

"Maybe."

"Did you divorce him?"

"Didn't have the money. I had two kids to raise. Your grandfather—the real one, your Grandfather Thornton—and I jumped the broom."

I puffed my cheeks out. This was better than the movies.

"His other wife. She white?"

"Yes." Grandmother turned the shirt over. "And his kids, all white. They live about 30 miles from here."

"No lie."

"Watch your mouth."

"I'm sorry."

Grandmother paused. "Sorry be as sorry does." The shirt was near to burning. "The white Parkers don't want to know you," she said flatly and began moving the iron back and forth again.

Chin cupped in my palms, I tried to imagine the white Parkers who'd never lay claim to me or my father. That year, 1961, Daddy went to court to prove he was the eldest son. He wanted the flag from his father's military coffin. He wanted his white brothers and sisters to see and acknowledge him.

Much later I found out Lieutenant Parker died of liver failure. Drank himself to death.

When my mother came to claim me, I didn't want to go. But since she and my father were trying marriage one more time, I had little choice. We were the only African-American family in a suburban white community. The community was fine. But Mother, unfortunately, was skittish that we'd seem too rowdy, which meant, in her mind, too colored. The first night, she laid down rules, soft yet insistent commands about propriety, about being pretty in a dull, not-flamboyant way. "Be charming. Be gracious," she said.

At 16 I grew rebellious. I was both a hippie and a power-to-the-people child. *"Times, they are a'changing"*... *"Say it loud, I'm black and I'm proud."*

I painted my bedroom red and black, hung fishnets from the ceiling, propped African spears and masks against the wall. A strobe light flickered in the corner, making every movement seem like two. Jimi Hendrix and the Jefferson Airplane blared from my stereo. I was celebrating my bloodlines, and for me, a black flower child was not a contradiction. I wore a bushy Afro and leopard prints with love beads and a lei. My Huey Newton print scared my mother more than the incense. My support of the Olympians' black-power salute frightened her more than the potential of my doing hard drugs at a pool party in a neighbor's back yard.

Mother kicked me out of the house. "Go," she said; Father said nothing. I flew from California back to Pittsburgh, to my birthplace, to Grandmother and Grandfather Thornton.

I think now that my mother couldn't accept herself. It was as though her shame that her family came from a plantation, that her grandmother was a mixed child of rape, still unsettled her. There was no lens to make the past less frightening, less upsetting to her sense of decorum. She wasn't an Uncle Tom or a white wanna-be. Rather, she was proud of her racial heritage, but her pride was bound up with the etiquette of a white world that was a figment of the '50s. Like Booker T. Washington, Mother thought if she worked hard enough, adopted the tastes of white middle-class culture, then she would be accepted. This desire for acceptance was her weakness, an insidious insecurity, an illogical belief that what she was—a mixed-blood, New-World African-American—was something to be ashamed of.

I say what she was was just fine. A special mix of humanity shaped my mother as it shaped and continues to shape us all. Mother's fears wouldn't let her embrace all the recesses and twists of her blood. Instead she established categories that contradicted themselves: Being black was fine; being a descendent of slaves was not fine. Being lovely like Lena Horne was fine; being descended from a white Master wasn't. If she could she would have suppressed half the blood that made her.

Sometimes I dreamed Mother and I were sitting on the bed, side by side, reflected in a wardrobe mirror. "See," she'd say to me. "You look just like me."

And I would nod, saying, "There's plenty of good ghosts in our blood."

"Yes," she'd answer, and just like a child's (a Native American's?) ritual of bonding, we'd prick our fingers, press them flesh to flesh, blood to blood, swearing, "Always." Swearing our ties couldn't be unbound. But I woke knowing Mother would have preferred purity. Being of mixed blood was too complicated for her. From either racial side, she thought she was being judged, could never be at ease. Her behavior became more and more rigid. Friendships, familial relations became a trial.

Mother surfaced periodically in my life, most memorably when she questioned the wisdom of my marrying a white man (Lucy's pale child from the North: British, Norwegian and Scotch-Irish). "Think of the children," she said.

True to form Mother did not call or write to congratulate me when I gave birth to a daughter. Nor did she call or write to congratulate me when I gave birth to a son.

One child light. One child dark.

My greatest fear is that one day someone will shout out to my son, "Nigger, what are you doing with that white girl?"

In the meantime I tell them to celebrate rivers, the roar of people, faces, histories stirring in their blood.

My census category is African-American. It always has been. Yet this category doesn't deny all the people in my blood, my genes, bubbling beneath my skin. I pass it all on. That's what Grandmother taught me.

In the 2000 census, millions of Americans checked more than one ethnic category. Native American. Hispanic. Anglo. Pacific Islander.

I think this is a good thing. All blood runs red.

Jewell Parker Rhodes is the author of three novels, "Voodoo Dreams," "Magic City" and "Douglass' Women" and of "The African American Guide to Writing and Publishing Nonfiction." Her work has appeared in Ms. Magazine and other popular and literary publications, and has been anthologized in "Children of the Night: Best Short Stories by Black Writers" and "Ancestral House: The Black Short Story in the Americas and Europe." Rhodes has been nominated twice for the Pushcart Prize and has won fellowships from Yaddo and the National Endowment for the Arts. She resides in Scottsdale, Ariz., where she is professor of creative writing and American literature at Arizona State University.

Prayer Dogs

Terry Tempest Williams

Prairie dogs. Prairie gods. Pleistocene mammals standing on their hind legs in the big wide open.

What do they see?

What do they smell?

What do they hear?

What they hear is the sound of a truck coming toward their town, the slamming of doors, the voices, the pressure of feet walking toward them. What they see now inside their burrow is the well-worn sole of a boot, now the pointed toe of the boot kicking out the entrance to their burrow, blue Levi's bending down, gloved hands flicking a lighter, the flame, the heat, then the hands shoving something burning inside the entrance. Something is burning. They back up farther down their tunnel, smoke now curling inside the darkness as the boot is kicking dirt inside, closing their burrow, covering their burrow, tamping the entrance shut. They are running down, down, down, around. They cannot see. What they smell is fear, fear in the form of gas. They cough and wheeze, their eyes burning, their lungs burning, tightening, cramping. They try to run, try to turn, nowhere to turn, every one of them scurrying to escape, to flee, but all exits have been kicked closed. The toxic smoke is chasing them like an invisible snake promising an agonizing death, suffocation, strangulation, every organ in spasm, until they collapse into each other's bodies, noses covered in blankets of familiar fur, families, young and old, slowly, cruelly gassed to death.

The truck drives away. The American flag is waving, the red-white-and-blue banner in the American West that says the rights of private landowners take precedence over the lives of prairie dogs who are standing in the way of development.

Above ground, all quiet on the Western front.

Below ground, a massacre.

Nearly 400 Utah prairie dogs disappeared in the summer of 1999 at the Cedar Ridge Golf Course. It is believed they were murdered, gassed to death. Two federal agents have been investigating the crime. This is a federal criminal offense. Penalties for killing or attempting to kill the federally protected animals range from fines of up to $100,000 to one year in prison. Some say the locals know who did it and are glad they did. Other locals are outraged. Both sides have offered rewards. One group has agreed to post bail for the offender; the other has offered a reward for the offender's arrest.

Gone. The prairie dogs are gone. Praise the Lord. Say it again with the Utah accent, "Praise the Lard." Fat. Fat Cats. Money. Money in the bank. The golf course, emerald green, with perfectly cropped lawn, is the crown jewel of the town in desert country.

Almost two years have passed. Nothing has been resolved. No one is talking. The Incident at Cedar Ridge has been all but forgotten. Cedar City takes pride in being a clean, wholesome town.

Utah prairie dogs, *Cynomys parvidens*, numbered more than 95,000 in the 1920s. By the 1960s their distribution was greatly reduced, the result of intensive poison-control campaigns administered by the Department of Agriculture, indiscriminate shooting, disease and loss of habitat. By the 1960s it was estimated that only 3,300 Utah prairie dogs in 37 separate colonies remained and that the species would be extinct by the year 2000. Because of the dramatic decline in its numbers and distribution, the species was classified as endangered on June 4, 1973. In the year 2000, the Utah prairie dog did not become extinct, but it continues to be threatened. Their numbers now are estimated at 4,582 individuals. Sixty-five percent of the population lives in Iron County, Utah. Eighty-six percent of all Utah prairie dogs live on private lands. The situation grows increasingly contentious between ranchers in southern Utah who want them exterminated because "the dogs are ruining the range," outside developers who want to cash in on the value of these open lands, and the federal agencies who must administer the Endangered Species Act. The hostile environment is fueled even further by the fact that southern Utah is one of the fastest-growing areas in the American West.

Iron County Commissioner Gene Roundy said, "I think it's a crime against society that a prairie dog can move into your front yard and you can't take care of it."

Whose society?

The South African poet Breyten Breytenbach writes, "The real revolutionary question is 'What about the Other?'"

There is a lion with his mouth open. I walk through it and enter TOTE-EM-IN, a roadside attraction off Carolina Beach Road in Wilmington, N.C. We are on vacation. Having worked in a natural history museum for over a decade, I am eager to learn what they may house inside. The interstate zoo boasts of having "over 100 exotic animals in a Dr. Dolittle atmosphere where you can 'talk with the animals.'"

The list is impressive: alligator, snapping turtle, painted turtle, box turtle, cottonmouth, king snake, corn snake, green rat snake, copperhead, spur-thighed tortoise, squirrel monkey, weeper capuchin, mandrill, jaguar, binturong, peccary, palm civet, kinkajou, python, black leopard, golden spider monkey, black spider monkey, Himalayan bear, Siberian tiger, Bennett's wallaby, Sitka deer, nilgai, camel, Patagonian cavy, zebra, aoudad, prairie dogs—my eye stops at a hometown species as the list continues.

"Where are your prairie dogs?" I ask the woman behind the counter of the gift shop inside.

"Out in back," she says. "We had two of our own and took two others in that belonged to someone else. We tried to slowly introduce them to one another, but it didn't work out."

"What do you mean?" I ask.

"I mean there are a lot of people who love prairie dogs, but they are more than they can handle; they're wild, after all. Some college students had them in their apartment, and the prairie dogs got out and made new tunnels in the heating ducts between apartments and escaped. They eventually found them and brought them to us, but they didn't get along with ours." She pauses. "It didn't work out—they died."

The woman is Sherrie Brewer. She and her husband, Jerry, run TOTE-EM-IN Zoo—bought it several years ago from George Tregemo, who started the zoo in 1952. Sherrie has kind eyes. Bucket in hand, she is on her way to feed the animals. "Come on out," she says. "I'll take you to the prairie dogs."

Wearing an orange, knitted cap and a camouflage jacket, she pours the contents of the bucket into a yellow wheelbarrow, then lifts the wheelbarrow and steers it down the gravel aisle lined with cages on either side.

We walk past the squirrel monkeys and two black panthers pacing back and forth.

"Some weather we've had," she says. "Record snowstorms for North Carolina this month, after a siege of hurricanes last summer."

Sherrie stops at a hay-lined cage on wheels, 6 feet tall, maybe 4 feet wide, and makes kissing sounds with her lips.

"Where you at, little guy? You're hidden real good now, aren't you?"

We wait.

"It doesn't say much for us that we spread out so much and ruin all their natural habitat, and this is where these animals end up, does it?" she says.

The guinea hens are crying for more food. Peacocks in the background are yelling, *Halp! Halp!*

"There he is," she says. "Hi, little guy."

We bend down and I see a prairie dog peeking out from a garbage can that is turned on its side and covered with hay. He scurries back in.

"How old do you think he is?" I ask.

"Probably 2 years."

We wait a few more minutes.

He comes out again, walks toward me, sniffing, stands upright, nose twitching, tail vibrating like a metronome. A tractor comes toward the cart. The prairie dog runs back into the can and turns his back.

"I'll leave you alone. If you need anything, I'll be over by the cats."

In time the prairie dog comes back out and climbs the side of the cage, his fingers with long, black nails grasping the chain links. I move closer and crouch down, eye to eye. This is the closest I have ever been to a prairie dog. It is also the only one I have seen in captivity.

My first impulse is to offer him something, anything. Without thinking, I click my tongue and offer my finger, which he takes. He just keeps staring. Eyes. His eyes. Black, unwavering eyes, like dark suns rising.

The characteristic mask is faded, a slight dusting of brown against beige. The black tip on his tail gives the species away. This is not a Utah prairie dog but a black-tailed prairie dog indigenous to the plains.

Suddenly he jumps down and begins chewing on hay, holding a piece in both hands. He is the color of dry grasses in the prairie, the desert, perfectly camouflaged, even in the hay.

Another visitor arrives. "How's my boy? How's my little boy, my little prairie-dog boy?"

The prairie dog climbs back up the side of the cage, and the man, obviously a regular, pokes his fingers inside to pat his stomach.

"Yes, that feels good, doesn't it? What a good boy. What a sweet boy, yes, yes. You don't get your belly rubbed every day, do you? Oh, yeah, yeah, that's my sweet prairie-dog boy."

The prairie dog puts his cheek against the chain link and closes his eyes as the man continues to rub his stomach.

"I come here a lot," the man says.

Prairie dogs out—standing on mounds all along I-70 from Grand Junction, Colo., to Cisco, Utah, just 25 miles from home. It's been a mild winter.

Sentinels. Up on their haunches. Arms folded. Some barking. Some foraging. Some running from mound to mound, their bodies rippling through the grasses. Others standing guard. Eagles may be near.

Today I am surprised by how large they seem. I keep thinking of the little one in North Carolina, held captive, his willingness to have his belly rubbed, his shy sociability, the brightness and intelligence of his eyes in spite of his surroundings, a cart of straw and a garbage can turned sideways.

Lewis and Clark wrote in 1804, during their journey west, this "wild dog of the prairie ... appears here in infinite numbers." Naturalist Ernest Thompson Seton estimated that prairie dogs numbered 5 billion in North America in the early 1900s. The largest prairie-dog colony on record, in Texas, measured 100 miles wide and 250 miles long and contained an estimated 400 million prairie dogs.

Today the headlines in the Rocky Mountain News read, "Little Help for Prairie Dogs." In Colorado 98 percent of the prairie-dog population is gone, as Colorado's Front Range is being developed from Boulder to Colorado Springs at an alarming rate. The U.S. Fish and Wildlife Service wants to list the black-tailed prairie dog as threatened, but they have no money for enforcement. Meanwhile developers of subdivisions and shopping malls are buying up land containing prairie-dog towns as fast as possible, having them removed by companies such as Dog Gone (*dog suckers*, they are called, who come and vacuum the prairie dogs up into the back of an enclosed truck with padded walls, then release them outside of town or sell them as ferret food), and starting to build immediately, before any protective measure might make any further development against the law.

What the spotted owl is to the old-growth forests in the Pacific Northwest, the prairie dog is to the grasslands and prairies of Middle America. The prairie dog has become another "indicator species," sounding the alarm for a disappearing ecosystem. The difference, however, between the owl and the prairie dog is the difference of perception: owls are symbols of wisdom; prairie dogs are varmints.

There are five species of prairie dogs in North America: black-tailed, white-tailed, Gunnison, Mexican and the Utah prairie dog. All of them are sociable creatures. All of them are seriously threatened.

Prairie dogs evolved in the Pleistocene Era and now represent the last of the Great Frontier. Historically prairie-dog towns followed the bison, aerating the soil after the great stampedes. These towns could range in size from one to 1,000 acres. Many in the Great Plains seemed to spread as far as the horizon. Within these communities are family units called *coteries*. A coterie, consisting of a single adult male, one to four adult females, and offspring up to 2 years old, can occupy a territory up to about an acre.

As above, so below. One could consider the double life of prairie dogs.

Above ground, prairie-dog colonies literally change the land. Mounds created from the excavation of burrows may be 2 feet high and 10 feet in diameter. These serve as lookout posts and will keep the burrows dry from rain. Their communication system is sophisticated. Biologists have identified 12 different vocalizations and a variety of postures and behavioral displays. One researcher studying a Utah prairie-dog population near Bryce Canyon National Park noted specific calls, distinguishing between the calls made when a truck versus a coyote crossed into their territory. When danger is near, a series of barks occur in a prairie-dog chorus, often led by sentinel dogs guarding the periphery of the colony. The word spreads. They quickly scramble and scurry across the desert and disappear into nearby holes. When danger seems to have passed, a prairie dog will carefully emerge, look in all directions, then stand on its mound and throw back its head, with its hands raised in what looks like a gesture of prayer, and give what has been called a *jump-yip* call that the coast is clear.

It is also common to see prairie dogs engage in what looks like kissing. The "kiss" is used to distinguish one coterie member from another. When prairie dogs recognize each other, they will participate in elaborate grooming behavior. If one of the prairie dogs is an intruder, teeth may be bared, territory fought over, claimed or reclaimed by dominant males. In most cases the outsider flees.

Below ground, a burrow will typically be 3 to 6 feet deep and about 15 feet long, although the size varies tremendously, depending on the landscape. Prairie dogs will often dig small chambers to the side of the main burrow where they can listen to what is going on above. Deeper inside the burrows, they make nests out of grasses they have pulled under, where they will sleep, give birth, and care for their young (four is the norm) in spring, with the babies usually not emerging until June. Native grasses comprise 70 to 95 percent of their diet during the summer, changing to seeds and insects, even roots, as fall and winter approach. Unlike other members in the ground-squirrel family, prairie dogs do not hibernate but rather lie dormant inside their network of burrows.

Prairie dogs create habitat not only for themselves but also for other grassland species. With their mounds and extensive burrowing systems (black-tailed prairie dogs typically have 30 to 50 burrow entrances per acre, while Gunnison's and white-tailed prairie dogs have fewer than 20), their underground world is not simply the haunt of prairie dogs but home to myriad other creatures, as well. One study of black-tailed prairie dogs identified more than 140 species of wildlife associated with prairie-dog towns, including bison, pronghorn antelope, burrowing owls, pocket mice, deer mice, ants, black widow spiders and horned larks, and many predators, such as rattlesnakes, golden eagles, badgers, bobcats, weasels, foxes, coyotes and black-footed ferrets.

In a grassland community historically tamped down by the weight of stampeding bison, burrowing prairie dogs loosen and aerate the soil, keeping the land supple. In the spring and summer, they also spend most of their time foraging above ground. A single prairie dog may consume 2 pounds of green grasses and forbs per week. Their hunger alters the landscape.

Prairie dogs' digging and scratching stimulates the soil, creating greater opportunities for seeds to germinate. With heightened water drainage due to the tunnels, plants grow. Plant diversity follows. Animal diversity follows the plants. Meadowlarks appear with an appetite for grasshoppers. Grasshopper sparrows appear in the abundance of seeds. Vacant or abandoned prairie-dog burrows become the homes of cottontails, kangaroo rats and deer mice. Burrowing owls, with their long, spindly legs, stand on the former mounds of prairie dogs with an eye for the multiplying mice. One successful life inspires another, creating the strength of a grassland community. If the prairie dog goes, so goes an entire ecosystem, including the black-footed ferret and burrowing owl, which now are endangered and threatened species.

Prairie dogs create diversity. Destroy them, and you destroy a varied world.

On my desk I have a small constellation of bones bleached by the sun. They belong to prairie dog: a skull with the jaw intact, two femur bones about the length of my little finger and two tibia, one broken in half. Alkaline sand from the Cisco desert still shakes out of the tiniest pores and teeth.

What is distinctive about this skull is the size of the eye socket. It is enormous in proportion to the rest of the skull. What does this vulnerable and venerable being see?

Niles Eldredge, a curator at the American Museum of Natural History, writes:

> *We are living amid a sixth extinction, one that, according to the Harvard biologist E.O. Wilson, is costing the earth some 30,000 species a year. Biologists estimate that there are at least 10 million species on earth right now. At this rate, the vast majority of the species on earth today will be gone by the next millennium.*

What are we to do?

The prairie dog is not a charismatic species, not a grizzly bear or wolf or whale. It is a rodent. We have gassed prairie dogs, poisoned them, and used them as targets. My own family calls them *pop guts*, which is what happens when you shoot them in the stomach. Their bodies are left to rot. They are expendable, despised, a lowly caste of animals, "the untouchables."

A headline in the March 7, 2001, edition of the Denver Post reads: "Judge Limits Kill to Prairie Dog." The article explains that a district judge has issued a temporary restraining order halting the extermination of a prairie-dog colony because of the danger to other animals. A state law protects all animals except rodents and birds from poisoning and trapping.

The issues circling the Utah prairie dog are the same ones shaping politics and culture in the American West. How do we define justice? How do we view progress? What kind of world do we want to maintain, and what kind of world do we want to create? Is economics the only standard by which we measure society's values? Or is it possible to adopt another ethical structure that extends our notion of community to include a compassion toward all species?

The fate of the prairie dog is caught in the middle of an ethical war: traditional farming and ranching practices, continued growth and sprawl versus ecological sustainability. Bull's-eye. Hit or miss?

What will we miss?

In 1950 government agents proposed to get rid of prairie dogs on some parts of the Navajo reservation in order to protect the roots of the sparse desert grasses and thereby maintain some marginal grazing for sheep. The Navajo elders objected, insisting, "If you kill all the prairie dogs, there will be no one to cry for the rain."

The amused officials assured the Navajo there was no correlation between rain and prairie dogs and carried out their plan. The outcome surprised only the federal officials. The desert near Chilchinbito, Ariz., became a virtual wasteland with very little grass. Without the ground-turning process of the burrowing animals, the soil became solidly packed, unable to accept rain. Hardpan. The result: fierce run-off whenever it rained. What sparse vegetation there was, was carried off by flooding waters.

J.M. Coetzee, in "The Lives of Animals," creates a character named Elizabeth Costello, a novelist, who defends the rights of animals before a skeptical university audience. She says, "There is no limit to the extent to which we can think ourselves into the being of another."

A professor of philosophy, Dr. Thomas O'Hearne, responds, "We may certainly wish for there to be community with animals, but that is not the same thing as living in community with them. It is just a piece of prelapsarian wistfulness."

Readers familiar with Coetzee's work as a South African writer know the passionate stance against apartheid, racism and specism that appear in such novels as "Waiting for the Barbarians" and "Disgrace."

Coetzee writes of a dream:

> *In the dream I stand again in a pit. The earth is damp, dark, water seeps up, my feet squelch, it costs me a slow effort to lift them.*
>
> *I feel under surface, searching for the bones. My hand comes up with the corner of a jute sack, black, rotten, which crumbles away between my fingers. I dip back into the ooze. . . . A dead bird, a parrot: I hold it by the tail, its bedraggled feathers hang down, its soggy wings droop, its eye sockets are empty. When I release it, it falls through the surface without a splash. "Poisoned water," I think. "I must be careful not to drink here. I must not touch my right hand to my mouth."*

A poisoned world. We are living in an increasingly toxic world, not just physically but emotionally. It is not a comfortable connection to make for most people: the ill-treatment of human beings and the mistreatment of animals. Both responses belong to arrogance, a lack of respect for life in all its diversity and complexity. We would rather not think too much about "what is being done to those outside the sphere of the favored group," yet I believe we can make a strong case for the extension of our empathy toward "the Other."

Schopenhauer writes:

> *Boundless compassion for all living beings is the firmest and surest guarantee of pure moral conduct, and needs no casuistry. . . . May all living beings remain free from pain.*

I think about my encounters with prairie dogs, both inside a cage and in the wild. I think about what they know in their bodies that has nothing to do with morals or ethics or any manner of abstractions, how they sing and chatter, kiss and caress and groom each other's fur, the interactions within their own families and the community at large, all this in the high desertlands of Utah, where eagles stand watch and coyotes skirt the periphery of prairie-dog towns. They are surviving, and given half a chance, they will survive us.

I believe prairie dogs know joy and fear and love and pain and that it is communicated within their tribe from every muscle and multiplying cell. All one has to do is stand on a bluff and listen to prairie dogs call back and forth to one another—this midday chatter, alongside meadowlarks and grasshoppers. Prairie dogs respond with their bodies, not with reason. It is a kinetic encounter, not an abstract one.

Call it instinct.

Call it "embodied knowledge."

Call it survival.

Prairie dogs know when they are safe, and they know when they are in danger.

Do we?

The Incident at Cedar Ridge haunts me. That boot, that hand, that hand that lit the cartridge of gas and shoved it inside the burrow of the prairie-dog town and allowed them to "disappear" is my own hand if I choose to do nothing in the wake of those murders.

I want to live and love in a varied world. I want to encounter Prairie-Dog People, Bear People, Raven People, Deer People, too, in the wild and near our homes and not be embarrassed by feelings of kinship that in our cynical world are viewed as sentimental.

"One sort of love does not need to block another," Mary Midgley writes in "Animals and Why They Matter," "because love, like compassion, is not a rare fluid to be economized, but a capacity which grows by use."

I cannot imagine the loneliness and cultural isolation we will suffer if we choose to live only in a world of our own making.

Without the diversity of the other-than-human world, without the individual intelligences and grace of other animals, our own intelligence and imagination are diminished.

We, too, are animals. We have evolved together. We evolved even with prairie dogs during the Pleistocene Era. Can we not continue our shared evolution, even the evolution of our own compassion? To deny our own animalness is to deny our both humble and powerful place in the scheme of life.

How do we wish to live, and with whom?

Once when I was walking the land near my home, a neighbor came up to me and said, "Have you seen any of them prayer dogs lately?"

"No," I said. "Not here."

"Damn if they didn't used to be a nuisance."

Terry Tempest Williams, author, naturalist and environmental activist, is perhaps best known for writing "Refuge: An Unnatural History of Family and Place," a classic in American nature writing. Her other books include "An Unspoken Hunger," "Desert Quartet: An Erotic Landscape," "Coyote's Canyon" and "Pieces of White Shell: A Journey to Navajoland," and two children's books, "The Secret Language of Snow" and "Between Cattails." Her work has appeared in The New Yorker, Nation, Outside, Audubon, Orion, Iowa Review, New England Review and other national and international publications. She has been a fellow for the John Simon Guggenheim Memorial Foundation and received a Lannan Literary Fellowship in Creative Nonfiction. Williams lives in Castle Valley, Utah.

Leaving Babylon:
A Walk Through the Jewish Divorce Ceremony
Judyth Har-Even

Two years after Cyrus, King of Persia, conquered the Babylonian Empire, he allowed the Children of Israel to return to their land. The year was 537 BCE. Two thousand five hundred and thirty-six years later, I walk down his street in Jerusalem, on my way to get divorced at the district rabbinic court. The travel agencies on Cyrus Street are not advertising group tours to Iraq, not yet. Nonetheless, Babylon is on my mind. By its rivers we sat down and wept when we remembered Zion and wondered how we could sing the Lord's song in a strange land. I wept and wondered, too, for 27 years of married life. Now, just as the Children of Israel walked back to their homeland, their freedom, I am walking to mine.

If all goes well at the courthouse this morning, I will receive my *get*, a Jewish writ of divorce. I already have a civil-divorce document, signed and stamped by an Israeli judge from the district family court. But to remarry in Israel, where I live, and to have "Divorced" rather than "Married" written on my identity card, I need the *get*. Only this document states categorically that I am divorced according to the Law of Moses and Israel.

The civil divorce derives from the decree of a civil court. The Jewish divorce derives from a ceremony steeped in tradition, played out by husband and wife in a rabbinic court. Friends have told me that the *get* ceremony, to which I am walking, is demeaning, primitive and meaningless.

Demons flitter and play along the narrow hallways of Jerusalem's rabbinic court. They are waiting to snatch a soul. Rabbinic legend claims that when people—women, especially—are in transition from one stage of life to another, demons get restless. Since the rabbinic

court is the venue for changing one's personal status, the building is a
playground for demons. Watch out, the Talmudic sages warned. Break
a glass at weddings; walk around the groom seven times; read Psalms;
wear amulets—anything to keep away the evil spirits.

I weave my way through the hallways and arrive intact at the
waiting room of Hall A. Other than Psalms, there are no instructions
for the soon-to-be-divorced, save for two signs on the door to the
courtroom: *Turn off your cellular phone*, and *Dress modestly*. I pick up
Psalms, open it randomly to Number 13, and read:

> *How long will I have cares on my mind, grief in my heart all day?*
> *How long will my enemy be exalted over me?*
> *Look and hear me, O Lord my God:*
> *Restore the luster to my eyes, lest I sleep the sleep of death…*

I am wearing a long, black skirt, a white blouse with sleeves that
cover my lascivious elbows, and a black sun hat. When my husband
enters the room and sees me dressed in uncharacteristically ultra-
modest garb, reading Psalms, he chides, "Who the fuck are you kidding?"

*I am sitting at home by myself, reading the newspaper by the light of one
lamp. There is a knock at the door. It is snowing outside, but I can't see the
snow because black paper is still taped to the windows. The Yom Kippur War
has been over for two months. My husband, a paratrooper, is still stationed in
Goshen. Before the war we were trying to make a baby, but now with his
being mobilized, there is no chance. My eggs escape unnoticed, untouched. The
snow has closed all the roads to Jerusalem.*

The knocking persists.

*All day I work with bereaved families. As a volunteer social worker for
the Ministry of Defense, I help mothers mourn their sons, widows their husbands, children their fathers. I am afraid to open the door, because I know it
could be a team of soldiers saying to me, "Your husband is dead."*

*The knocking persists. I walk to the door. I open it. A man stands there
in a green uniform covered with mud and snow. He holds an M16 in one
hand and 10 red roses in the other.*

"Ovulate yet?" he asks.

An usher calls out our last name and escorts us into the chamber.
Opposite the door, towering above us, is a long, Formica desk. Behind
it, three rabbinic judges sit ensconced on cushioned chairs. They wear

costumes—black jackets, white shirts, gray beards and black hats with flat rims. The rabbi on the left is immersed in reading a tome and does not look up when we enter the courtroom. The rabbi on the right is sucking his thumb. He avoids my incredulous stare, which he would have to interpret as lecherous, versed as he must be in rabbinic wisdom. The judge in the middle looks at my husband and me as if our whole, sad history is incised on our foreheads.

To the left of the long desk is a small, green Formica desk with a computer. Here sits the court secretary. He is a kindly-looking man, bald, with a skullcap.

"Has your w-w-witness arrived?" the attentive rabbi asks.

"Yes," I respond.

"Tell her to come in and then be seated."

I do as I'm told. Nechama, my witness, is an observant Jew from my hometown in the United States. She has played this role for other divorcing friends.

Act 1: The Name

"Do you know this woman's f-f-father?" the rabbi asks Nechama.

"Yes. I knew him."

The rabbi listens as if this is the most important information he has heard since his political party became the second largest in Israel.

"Was he a C-C-Cohen?"

"I don't know."

Now the rabbi leans over his desk to question me.

"Did your father ever tell you he was a C-C-Cohen?"

My thoughts race to Moses, the prophet who stuttered. I repress a smile. My father didn't even know what a Cohen was.

"Never," I say.

We are both surprised at the discrepancy in the religious documents. Apparently my name on the *ketuba*, the marriage contract, says I am the daughter of a Cohen. The marriage certificate, however, issued by the Ministry of Religious Affairs after the wedding, says I am a daughter of Israel.

For the purposes of personal status, Jews are divided into two categories: Cohen, the priestly class, and Israel, the rest. I always thought I was one of the rest, but now it appears I may belong to the priestly class.

"What name was used when your father was called up to the T-T-Torah?" the rabbi demands.

A Jewish name, for purposes of marriage and divorce, consists of a given name, the given name of one's mother and father, and the father's religious class, that is, Cohen or Israel. This is why we are spending 20 minutes trying to figure out who I am. Judyth? Judy? Yehudit? Cohen? Israel?

My precise name and lineage is of the utmost importance because the writ of divorce has to be written specifically for me. The legal principle that the *get* be written for a specific wife on a particular day derives from interpretations of the first two verses in Chapter 24, Deuteronomy:

> *When a man has taken a wife and married (possesses) her and it comes to pass that she no longer finds favor in his eyes, because he has found some unseemly thing in her, then let him write her a bill of divorce and give it in her hand and send her out of his house. And when she is departed out of his house, she may go and be another man's wife.*

This passage offered fertile soil for reams of rabbinic free associations and legalities, which were ultimately woven together in Tractate Gittin of the Babylonian Talmud, compiled in 500 CE. Talmudic sages deduced at least nine legal principles from the passage in Deuteronomy:

1.   *A man must divorce his wife of his own free will.*
2.   *A woman must be divorced in writing.*
3.   *The get must be a document that states clearly that it severs all ties between husband and wife.*
4.   *The husband must give the get to the wife. She cannot take it.*
5.   *He must put it in her hand. The woman is not divorced until the get comes into her possession.*
6.   *The document must state that he sends her out.*
7.   *The get must be given in the presence of two or three witnesses. (This is based on a common word—*davar*— "thing," which appears in Deuteronomy 24:1–2 and 19:15, where it refers to witnesses.)*
8.   *The get must be given immediately after it is written. (For instance, if a husband goes bowling after he writes the get or obtains it from a scribe, and then delivers it, the get is invalid, unkosher.)*

9.   The get *must be given only for the purpose of divorce; it cannot be used as a threat.*

"Was her father a C-C-Cohen?" the rabbi pleads again.

It is one hour before the wedding. The men are sitting around a table with the officiating Orthodox rabbi filling in the details of the ketuba. *The rabbi turns to my father.*
"What was the name you gave your daughter at birth?"
"She was christened Judy."
The other men, including my husband-to-be, cannot believe their ears. They motion my father to shut up.
"Christened?" *the rabbi repeats, eyebrows raised.*
"Yes. At birth we called her Judy."
"But . . . was she christened?"
"Oh, I don't know. That's what we called her."
"Was she christened?"
"What the hell difference does it make? You think every word is important? Let's just get her married, for Christ's sake."

"Who was the rabbi who officiated at your w-w-wedding?" This rabbi is desperate for details, where, some believe, God dwells.

"Rabbi Natan," I reply, "an Orthodox rabbi from Jerusalem." I emphasize this last point so he will understand that someone in his own Orthodox establishment screwed up in 1972.

The talking rabbi looks at the reading rabbi, who points at his watch and urges him to proceed.

The rabbi decides that I am an Israel, thanks my witness, and dismisses her. Then he calls my husband's witness. The man is a jerk. He makes light of my husband's many nicknames. The rabbi reminds him this is serious business, chooses two names among the many, and sends him away after a 10-minute interrogation.

At this juncture a cellular phone in my husband's briefcase rings. The judges and court secretary take cover, as if a knife-wielding terrorist has burst into the room.

"Didn't you read the sign?" the rabbi yells. "Turn that thing off. A little respect for the court, please."

I wonder if Moses lost his stutter when he reprimanded the Children of Israel.

Act 2: The Players

The rabbi calls in two *shlubs*. Their shirttails hang over their black trousers, and their black skullcaps dangle from the sides of their heads. Tweedledee and Tweedledum are full-time employees of the Ministry of Religious Affairs, two of six men who play the role of witness at divorce proceedings. They enter from a side door like extras on a movie set, their only task to stand up, pay attention, and say "Yes" or "No" when asked. My taxes pay their salaries.

The two witnesses stand between the court secretary and the rabbis. Then the talking rabbi calls in my husband's emissary. Enter the Torah scribe. He is a short man wearing a white shirt with a frayed collar and a black skullcap placed on his bald head like a dot over an "i." He takes up his position opposite my husband. His props are a piece of parchment made from the skin of a kosher animal, a *kulmus*, or reed pen, and a small bottle of ink. The ink is made of crushed sap, pomegranate skin, gallnut and soot from burnt grapevines, all brewed in water for 12 hours. The exact recipe has been passed down from generation to generation for the past 1,600 years, give or take.

The drama begins when the rabbi tells the scribe to give his writing instruments to my husband.

"These are now y-y-yours," says the rabbi, looking at my husband. "Repeat after me: 'These are my writing implements.'"

My husband swallows his pride and intelligence to get out the sentence. "These are my writing implements."

"Speak up and take the gum out of your mouth."

My husband takes the gum out of his mouth and holds it in his right hand. Then he repeats, "These are my writing implements."

The rabbi swivels toward the witnesses and asks if they heard.

"Yes," they chirp.

Then he swivels back.

"Now give your writing implements to the Torah scribe and say, 'I am giving you my implements, and you will write the *get* for me.'"

"I am giving you my implements, and you will write the *get* for me," my husband whispers as he hands the writing materials to the scribe.

The rabbi turns to the scribe and asks, "Did he just give you these writing m-m-materials?"

Well-versed, the scribe produces a clear "Yes." Then the rabbi instructs the scribe, my husband and the two witnesses to retire to a separate room to write the *get*, the writ of divorce. I am dismissed for intermission.

A scribe writes the *get* on a parchment marked with a stylus. The text consists of 12 lines of Hebrew and Aramaic, 12 being the numerical value of the Hebrew letters *gimmel* and *tet*, which spell *get*. The exact wording was finalized by the Babylonian sages of the fourth century CE, who also laid down strict details for its calligraphy. The *get* could only be written in a city or town with a source of water.

This is the standard Jerusalem text, which my husband and the two witnesses watched the scribe write with his reed pen:

> On the ____ day of the week, the ____ day of the month _____, in the year _____ of the creation of the world, according to the number of years we count here in Jerusalem, on the waters of the Siloam Spring and by cistern waters, I, called _____, son of _____, called _____, standing today in Jerusalem, the city which has cisterns for water, do hereby consent with my own free will, without any duress, to free and release and divorce you, my wife, called _____, daughter of _____, called _____, standing today in Jerusalem, who has previously been my wife, and now I release and send away and divorce you so that you will be free to go and govern yourself and be married to any man you desire and let no person oppose you from this day and forever and behold you are permitted to every man. And this shall be for you from me a bill of divorce and an epistle of sending away and a bill of release according to the Law of Moses and Israel.
>
> _____, son of _____, witness
> _____, son of _____, witness

The Mishna, the code of Jewish law edited by Judah the Prince in Zippori, Lower Galilee, around 2000 CE, says that a husband can write the writ of divorce on the horn of a bull, but then the husband must hand his wife the whole bull. A husband or his scribe can write the prescribed lines on the hand of a slave, but then the wife gets the living, full-bodied slave. The rabbis argued over whether or not the writ of divorce could be written on an olive leaf. I think about these disputes as I wait for the final act of my *get* ceremony. My tradition often seems bizarre, ludicrous and surreal. These are the qualities that my friends warned me about, interpreting the ceremony as demeaning, primitive and meaningless. But this strangeness stems from the ceremony being rooted in a time when Jews owned slaves and scribes wrote on horns. Though part of me chuckles at the antics of the three rabbis this morning, another part acknowledges that the tradition is larger and richer than those rabbis who claim to be its guardians. Standing in front of the politically appointed rabbinic judges, I look beyond them and see the Israelites who walked out of Babylon and those who left Egypt. The Israelites came home from the North and from the South at different periods in my history. They came from the East and from the West throughout the centuries, all yearning to create a new life in a Promised Land.

We are all players in the same story. It is an ancient tale, told and retold, and though the ceremony this morning in 1999 seems absurd, I love it for the continuity it affords. Each jot and tittle holds me in place against torrents of upheaval. When pieces of my life shatter like shards, the tradition binds. Moreover, the same sages and texts that prescribe my Jewish divorce determined the ceremony in which I was wed, that in which my sons entered the Covenant and those that I enact every Sabbath and on holidays. It is that tradition, that Jewish sanctification of time, that provided the scaffolding for holding my family together for 27 years. Ironically it is that same tradition that allows me an out.

Jewish tradition accepts divorce as a necessary evil, evil because ideally a marriage parallels the eternal covenant between God and Israel. The prophet Malachi admonishes, "Let no one break faith with the wife of his youth. For I detest divorce, said the Lord, the God of Israel." Being human, however, the Talmudic sages recognized the difference between the ideal and the real. They understood that divorce was sometimes necessary, but they did not want to make it an easy procedure.

A kosher divorce cannot be derived by a simple, public statement of "You are no longer my wife." A valid divorce cannot be derived from one action—a husband sending out his wife from their home. The sages determined that a divorce, according to the Law of Moses and Israel, is valid only if a specific document is written in the presence of two witnesses and given to the wife in the presence of those same witnesses. The Talmudic sages hoped that the husband, while going through the involved process, would reconsider and not divorce.

Whereas God was present in my wedding ceremony, he is absent from the divorce proceedings. His name is neither mentioned nor invoked. I imagine him off in a corner, sulking, and for good reason. What, after all, has God been doing every day since the creation of the world? According to the Babylonian Talmud, he has been running a dating service, matchmaking, a task more difficult, the sages claim, than splitting the waters during the Exodus.

My tradition is the palace in which I play out universal themes. Encountering it here in the rabbinic court on a summer morning at the end of the second millennium, I feel as if I have been catapulted back to my roots. The penchant for detail springs from these rock-bottom roots.

I am fortunate that my husband is cooperating in granting me a *get*. Thousands of Jewish women are not so lucky. Called *agunot*, they are locked in unwanted, often violent marriages because their husbands refuse to grant them a *get*. For them the tradition is a prison. For me it is an ancient palace, rising out of a chaotic sea, a palace I visit at the most meaningful transitions of my life.

Act 3: The Walk

After 20 minutes my husband returns with the scribe and the witnesses. They are not smiling. The five of us walk back into the chambers.

The rabbi asks my husband if he is giving me this divorce of his own free will or if somebody is forcing him to do so. In Jewish tradition only the man can grant the woman a divorce. Even if the woman initiates the divorce, the man must say that he is willingly granting it. I hesitate. My husband could balk. He could scream, "It's all *her* idea. *She's* the one who left *me*. *She's* the one who's always taking the initiative. *I* didn't want to get married in the first place. It was *her* idea. It's all *her* fault."

The ambivalence in my heart would like him not to cooperate, at least for a minute. I would like to hear a refusal because it would be an acknowledgement that he cares. But he acquiesces, albeit softly.

"I can't hear you," the rabbi bellows.

"Yes, my own free will. Nobody is forcing me." He barely opens his lips.

We are standing under the wedding canopy in 1972. It is a warm, May evening—Lag B'Omer, the 33rd day of the counting of the barley offering in Jerusalem 2,000 years ago, and the only date between Passover and the Feast of Weeks when Orthodox Jewish weddings can take place. Two witnesses and my mother stand with us under the canopy. Tears squat in the corners of my mother's eyes. I see them when I walk around my fiancé seven times. After the seventh circle, I stop next to my man. He looks like a child who has been praised by his kindergarten teacher. He lifts my veil to give me a sip of wine. It is sweet and sanctified. Then he opens his lips slightly, just slightly, and takes a sip. God is crossing his fingers.

The rabbi turns to the witnesses. "Did you hear him?"

"Yes," they chant.

The scribe hands the parchment to my husband, who hands it to the rabbi, who folds it into sixths and hands it back to my husband. The parchment is like a hot potato. Nobody wants to hold it because it is human evidence that God failed. And if his matchmaking is faulty, what about his other interventions?

The rabbi tells my husband to say the following words to me: "Behold, this is your *get*. Accept it, for with it you will be divorced from me from this moment and be permitted to all men." My husband follows the rabbi's orders. He looks straight into my eyes.

"Behold, this is your *get*. Accept it, for with it you will be divorced from me from this moment and be permitted to all men."

The words freeze in the hot, July air. I cannot believe he is letting me go, sending me out to copulate with other men. We were enmeshed for so many years. How can he do this to me?

It is the first year of our marriage. Every night, I lie on top of my husband, who lies on the living-room couch and watches television. We are one flesh. Eventually I want to sit up. I even want to go into the other room to read a book. I go.

For weeks he does not respond when I talk to him. Over the years we try five marriage counselors. Nothing works. One night after 24 years of marriage, he throws a damp towel onto my desk.

"This was out of place," he shouts.
I ask him to leave.
"If you don't like it, lady, you know where the fuck you can go."

Now the rabbi tells me to hold my arms out toward my husband and cup my hands together, with my thumbs slightly inside the cups. I do as I am told.

"No, do not move your thumbs. Do not grab," he admonishes. "You are a vessel. Let the parchment fall into your hands. He must give it to y-y-you."

Now he directs my husband. "Hold the folded parchment about half a meter above her h-h-hands." My husband obeys.

"As soon as he drops it," the rabbi instructs me, "I want you to grasp it with two hands, like this." He holds his hands in the position of Christian prayer.

We both do as we're told. My husband drops the writ of divorce into my hands. I clutch the folded parchment.

"Did you see that?" the rabbi turns to ask the witnesses, who are still awake.

"Yes," they yawn.

"Now hold your hands in front of you, grasping the writ, and walk over th-th-there," he tells me, pointing to the far side of the room.

I am a good walker.

It is a Friday night, the Sabbath. We are seated at either end of the dining-room table, flanked by our three children. I have blessed the Sabbath candles; my husband has blessed the wine; our youngest son has blessed the bread. This is the only time during the week we sit together as a family. I want it to be pleasant, so I make conversation and encourage the children to speak. My hus-band watches the TV weekly news round-up. I hope he won't explode this week, when the wine spills on the tablecloth. I want it to be pleasant, a blessing.

As my 14-year-old daughter and I clear the soup plates — homemade veg-etable barley — she says to me, "Don't you see he doesn't love you?"

I control the tears through the homemade apple strudel and then run out the door, down the 64 stairs, up seven blocks, down two hills, over three neighborhoods, halfway to Bethlehem. I walk fast, tears streaming down my cheeks, arms swinging violently.

By the time I return to the living room an hour later, everyone is sitting in silence in front of the TV, watching the latest terrorist attack.

In the courtroom I take large, powerful strides, but the room, being small and crowded, is big enough only for three. I would crash through the wall if the rabbi told me to, but when I come up against the corner, he says to turn around and come back. I walk. I stand below the three rabbis, the folded parchment between my palms. The rabbi looks at me and says, "You are now a divorced woman. You are permitted to any m-m-man, and you can get married in 92 days. Please give me the parchment."

I hand the rabbi the document. He tears it slightly to assure that another couple with our exact names will not use this *get* today.

I say, "Thank you" and "Goodbye." The reading rabbi closes his book; the sucking rabbi extracts his thumb; and Moses wishes us good luck in our new lives.

When I say, "Thank you" and "Goodbye" to my ex-husband, his silent armor glistens.

Downstairs, outside, a smile breaks forth. It stretches from Cyrus Street to King Solomon Road. I walk over to King David Street and think what a pity these kings are dead, now that I am available and my self-esteem can handle royalty. Marriage, however, is not on my mind, despite the rabbi's mention of those 92 days. According to the calculations of the Talmudic sages, that is how long it will take to determine if I am pregnant. This is important, in order to determine the hypothetical fatherhood of the hypothetical fetus.

The King David Hotel on King David Street is bustling with activity. U.S. envoy Dennis Ross is in town trying to help Israelis and Palestinians piece together a separation agreement. Tourist buses block the road. I am glad I am not a tourist. The only place I want to go to is the land of self-respect, the land of my freedom. My feet will take me there. I turn onto Hebron Way. Cars, buses and ambulances race by as I walk out of bondage, leaving Babylon.

For our first anniversary, I want to buy him something special. He doesn't like jewelry. In fact he doesn't even wear a wedding ring. I choose the Encyclopedia Judaica and buy it on installments. I imagine my husband will be proud to own this rich compendium of Jewish knowledge.

On the eve of our anniversary, he opens the carton, looks, hesitates, and then closes it. He turns to me with disappointment.

"You really don't know who I am, do you?"

I turn onto Ein Gedi Street, where I live with solitude in a garden apartment. Suddenly, the earth whimpers; a soft hiss rises from the ground. From the North an unnatural dampness saturates the street. Sniffles and staccato breaths ride the hot, July air. I stop. I wipe tears from my cheeks and rub my fingers on the amulet around my neck.

I will miss Babylon, where I stayed too long. Even in a strange land, one learns to sing.

Like shards, the final words from Tractate Gittin scatter before me on the damp pavement. I pick them up and reconstruct the ancient truth, "When a man divorces the wife of his youth, even the altar sheds tears."

Judyth Har-Even has written personal essays for the Jerusalem Post, Israel's largest English-language daily, since 1984. Her essays and poetry have appeared in Kenyon Review, Hadassah Magazine, Lilith and Jewish newspapers in the United States and Canada. Her work has been anthologized in "Headway: A Thematic Reader" (Holt Rinehart & Winston 1970), "Jewish Possibilities: The Best of Moment Magazine," (Jason Aronson 1987) and "Mores of Our Lives: An Anthology of Jewish Women's Writings" (Targum/Feldheim 1993.) A native of Ohio, she received her bachelor's in American culture from the University of Michigan and her master's in creative nonfiction from Goucher College. She has lived in Jerusalem since 1967.

Lessons in Killing for the
Black Buddhist Nun

Faith Adiele

The proper mental attitude is vital for both general mindfulness and specific meditation ... meditation ends with a chant designed to cultivate the Four Sublime States of Mind: Mudita *(sympathetic joy for others' success),* Karuna *(compassion for all living beings who are suffering),* Upekkha *(facing vicissitudes with equanimity and calm), and* Metta *(universal love and good-will).*

— *Nyanaponika, "The Heart of Buddhist Meditation"*

*W*hen I was 5, my mother came home one Friday from the California junior high school where she taught and announced that she had a surprise. "A surprise?" I glanced over from my perch on the kitchen counter. She stood in the doorway, cheeks flushed pink from the heat, straw-colored hair clinging to her back. I hit the floor. "Where?"

"It's in my bag in the living—" she started as I shot past.

My mother was famous for her gifts. When we were living on lentils and rubbery, government-surplus cheese, she wrote storybooks about African girls like me, warrior-scholars who rescued indecisive princes, and painted her own illustrations. She dug through fabric-store bins for felt scraps to paste to the backs of the Ebony magazine models who populated my felt-boards. Once she found work, her quest for the perfect toy began in earnest. She could talk merchants out of anything marked Not for Sale, Display Only and routinely staggered off the bus lugging beaded tepees, African masks, boy dolls with tiny, plastic penises.

When necessary my mother revised the available world. She sewed African outfits out of faux leopard-skin for a village of black dolls. She took Tawny Taupe fingernail polish and black markers to my picture books and paper dolls, darkening the pink faces and pale hair to resemble mine. She replaced guns with plastic animals and tiny nets. I was a teen-ager before I realized that G.I. Joe was actually a soldier and not Dr. Mark Luther, Global Adventurer and Official Government Archeologist.

The afternoon of my mother's surprise, I rushed to our postage stamp of a living room. My mother's bag, a deep, straw tote with two loops for handles, perched in the rocking chair between a tower of student folders and a satchel bulging with books. Perhaps the surprise wasn't a toy at all. Perhaps one of her students had given her a batch of homemade tamales, still steaming in their corn husks, or perhaps she'd stopped at the bakery across the street and picked up one of the maple bars the counter lady always saved for me.

Years later I would learn that my sunny childhood neighborhood had been as carefully constructed as my mother's repainted toys. Our close-knit apartment complex and playground were actually a low-income housing project and a vacant lot. My long-standing love of mud pies was born of necessity, given the scarce grass. My bakery saint was a point person, paid 50 cents a week to reserve a maple bar and watch for me on my walk home from the babysitter's. And rather than preparing time-consuming delicacies, my mother's students were more likely to shadow her home, chanting "Nigger-lover" and pelting her white, 5-foot-2-inch frame with rocks.

But at 5, I knew nothing of this. Upon reaching my mother's beach tote, I yanked the handles apart and thrust my face inside. My nostrils skimmed the snake coiled asleep at the bottom. Too stunned to scream, I snapped my neck out of the bag and fell to the floor. Mouth pumping open and shut, I must have resembled the goldfish we'd tried raising, a doomed experiment of tiny gold and black shadows (leave it to my mother to find an equal number of black goldfish), who mouthed mysterious, pleading vowels from behind the thick magnification of their bowl before invariably, persistently turning their shimmery apricot and plum bellies to the ceiling.

After a minute I started hollering.

"Good God!" my mother exclaimed, hurrying out of the kitchen. "You'll scare the poor thing to death!" She dipped a pale, dimpled arm into the bag and it emerged, the snake molded to it like a jade-and-silver bracelet. An avenging goddess, she turned to me, the snake's flat head wavering in midair below hers. "Where did you learn this sort of behavior?" she demanded, the snake's black, forked tongue flickering at me like an accusatory echo.

Mudita *(Sympathetic Joy)*

While preparing for my vows, I find an ordination script in which the ordaining monk asks the postulant to swear that he is human. Over lunch I ask my teacher about this "being human" requirement.

Sweeping his chopsticks aloft like a conductor's baton, Ajarn Boon airlifts several fish balls out of his bowl and drops them into mine. He's like a Thai mother, covering the terrain with a barrage of delicacies.

"That's simple," he says. Plop, plop. "In ancient India there once was a naga, a great serpent, who took human form and ordained as a monk. He was a devout practitioner, but one night as he slept, his true form revealed itself. Sadly the Buddha forced him to disrobe, explaining that serpents could not ordain. He promised, however, that the naga's image would henceforth be placed in temples to honor his devotion."

This is why during the intermediary stage after a postulant has shaven his head but before he's taken his vows, he's referred to as Naga. The snake who exists in the realm between human and monk.

My host mother tells a different story. According to her, the snake king, Mucalinda, protected the Buddha from rain for seven days while he was deep in meditation. Hence the recurring image of a meditating Buddha seated atop a coiled snake with a cobra's hood behind him. The snake as human protector.

My texts claim that images of nagas date back to pre-Buddhist, snake-worshipping cults and were later incorporated into Hindu and Buddhist mythology. Nagas were semi-divine beings, half human, half snake, who could assume either form. They guard temple doors, appearing as hooded cobras with many heads, or human beings with a snake tail and canopy of hoods.

I'm haunted by the snake who wanted to ordain. Why, since he'd proven himself, couldn't he remain a monk? My Buddhist charts relegate all beings to fixed places in the cosmic hierarchy as determined by their karma. Lowest are hell sprites; next come hungry ghosts, then animals. Humans exist on a higher plane because we can stop the cycle of rebirth. At the top float various enlightened beings and gods.

So a snake is a snake for a reason. As a human he must have acted badly, damaging his karma enough for a lower birth. Only once he accrues enough merit to be reborn as human can he aspire to the next step—ordination. Humans build merit through good deeds, gifts to temples, parenting a monk. I wonder how snakes accrue theirs.

I understood my mother's surprise at my reaction to the snake. I was no stranger to animals, after all. After the suicidal goldfish came a stream of metamorphosing tadpoles: Tails emerged and dropped off; one leg appeared without the apparent need for a partner; an entire evolutionary cycle occurred over the course of a single night, with fully formed frogs crawling out of the primordial ooze of my Woolworth's Tabletop Tadpolium. Soon miniature turtles came to share the yellow, plastic island and rest under the ragged shade of its snap-on palm tree.

As my mother and I moved higher up the food chain, hamburger and the occasional pork chop appearing on our rickety, Formica dinner table, I graduated to mammals. For years I ran a futuristic city of white mice. Like most home-improvement projects, my plastic HabiTrail was always in mid-construction, soaking up my allowance with endless additions of red exercise wheels and yellow tunnels leading nowhere. On weekends I took the mice to Mom's bed, and as she read aloud from "On the Banks of Plum Creek," watched them tunnel beneath the blankets, busily creating furrows around our lazy legs.

When we moved to my grandparents' farm and stopped eating meat—this time by choice, Mom measuring out swirls of beans and mesas of rice according to "Diet for a Small Planet"—I finally got a real American pet, a puppy. And when, one day a few months later, I came home from a sleep-over to find that Laddie, whose eye had begun to bulge milky blue, had mysteriously disappeared, a gang of cats was there to replace him.

Then there were the animals we tried to save: the series of stray cats abandoned in irrigation ditches, on the side of the highway, or once word got out about the "Cat Lady," on our doorstep, whom we took to the vet for repairs, taught to trust again, and gave away. The spiders weaving mummified flies into dusty ceiling corners, whose execution my mother stayed by placing her chair beneath them. For hours she rocked, calmly reading, the spider spinning and dropping perilously close to her nest of cowlicks, while my grandmother patrolled the perimeter with a broom and dust rag, eyes glinting.

Finally there were the fish. Each summer my mother relinquished me to my grandparents, Old Pappa and Mummi, for camping trips, deer hunts, fishing parties, with the proviso that everything we killed would be consumed, necessary. My grandfather and I stood at the edge of the Pacific as the sun stained the sky shades of pink, and reeled in catch after catch of muscular fish effortlessly, despite the fact that summer-run steelhead always slammed the bait and tore up the river. Meanwhile all around us, fishermen squirmed, switching from casting to spin rods, checking reel capacity, fingering heavier fly lines with sink tips, their faces stretched in grimaces approximating smiles.

Later when we staggered back to the trailer, each toting a bucket teeming with fat, rose-bellied trout, Old Pappa roared with laughter. "All those grown men without a single bite between them watching this bitty girl pull 'em in and trying to be excited for her!"

I joined their laughter but shrieked when Mummi reached for my bucket. "No!"

My grandparents eyed each other. "But, *pulla*," Mummi tried to explain, "that's the whole point of fishing. And you love fried trout."

I draped myself over my bucket and sobbed.

"Okay, honey," Old Pappa conceded, "that's fine, but we should throw them back so they can live."

I sobbed all the more loudly.

And so the bucket remained outside our trailer, the silvery steelhead dulling to gray, moving in increasingly listless circles, until Mummi, one hand pinching her nose, handed me a bucket of corpses.

Karuna *(Compassion)*

Head nun Roongdüan says the most profound moment of her ordained life was her three-month thudong. Traditionally these "hard-practice" pilgrimages entail trips to the deep forest, mountain peaks or cremation sites for solitary, intensive meditation. I've never heard of a woman doing thudong.

She'd been invited to preach and decided to travel with four nuns from one end of Thailand to the other. Each took an umbrella, a mosquito net, an alms bowl and the clothes on her back. Deep in the Malay Peninsula, the villagers work nights stripping rubber trees and sleep days, when alms rounds traditionally happen. Since it's forbidden for an ordained person to eat after the sun reaches its zenith, this meant the nuns had to go for days without food. Often, sitting alone in an empty field, Roongdüan would come out of meditation to find cobras on either side of her— "coiled like little stupas*"—or with their heads in her lap, perhaps attracted by her body heat. She felt that they were being watched over by all creatures.*

That California afternoon my mother's surprise undulated across the summer-peach flesh of her arm. Mom clucked softly. "Really, punkin'," she said, "he's just a harmless little garter snake. You're so much bigger. How can you be scared of him?"

She held out her other arm, and the snake draped itself through space, freezing in mid-shape, wrapping her in its muscular embrace. "Don't you want to meet him?" she asked. "He's sweet. A student rescued him from a squirrel, and I asked if we could keep him over the weekend." She waved a glittering, scale-covered arm. "He knows how to play hide-and-seek."

"Really?" I crept forward. Three light-green stripes ran the length of the snake's body, marking a beaded pattern. It looked like a bolt of fine fabric pouring through her pearl-tipped fingers. "Is it slimy?"

"Of course not." She held out a coil. "He feels really neat."

I grinned, feeling foolish in the face of her enthusiasm, and poked a section far from the head with its darting, fissured tongue. The scales felt not like a fish's hard, articulated ones but smooth and cool, the way a water-worn stone fits snugly in the palm.

"See?" My mother nodded. "Not slimy." She knuckled several places where the scales rose up a good half-inch, forming miniature anthills. "We think he must have been bitten by the squirrel, poor thing."

My fingers trembled over the rise and descent of the bite. The snake seemed to smile, its mouth curved upward. "My student is keeping him until he recovers enough to go back to the wild."

My mother and I spent the day hiding behind our few pieces of furniture as the snake slithered across the napless carpeting after us, and the evening taking turns reading aloud from the snake books she'd brought from the school library. By the time I presented my Sunday homework report, I knew all about the 13 species of American garter snake, how the females are longer and thicker than the males, how they're drawn to parks and other human habitats, how the tongue acts as the nose, how they have no ears. I understood the garter's importance to our ecosystem, eating frogs and mice and keeping away its poisonous cousins.

But on Monday morning, as my mother, sighing, uncoiled the snake from her neck and settled him into the bottom of her bag, a thought flickered through my mind as quickly as the appearance and disappearance of that black, splintered tongue: Neither my delight in the snake's arrival nor my sadness at its departure equaled hers. True, I was capable of feeling such outrage on the behalf of mistreated creatures that I'd become physically ill, my stomach flaming as I passed scabby dogs on the ends of chains, yet I suspected that it wasn't the same as feeling true affection.

Perhaps it didn't matter. Perhaps the important thing was that by age 5, I had internalized my mother's code of behavior. I had a crippling sense of compassion and a yearning for others' self-determination. I set as impossibly high standards for myself as for others. So what if I lacked what the Buddhists call *metta*, true love?

For years to come, I would champion the scabby dog. As a child I collected signatures, formed volunteer organizations, dragged home worm-eaten kittens, and visited nursing homes, steeling myself against the smell. In college I mastered a rhetoric of empowerment and social justice, theorizing grassroots development projects and skipping class to teach English to refugees. After graduating I worked a series of low-paying jobs in human services, legalizing undocumented immigrants, mentoring inner-city girls, smuggling activists out of Burma, plying needy students with Hershey's Kisses and sympathy. I was despairing of humanity, outraged at middle-class complacency, inspired by the level of my colleagues' commitment, shamed by my own. I acted and I behaved, always hoping, as the Jewish adage reassures, that by going through the motions, faith would surely follow.

Karuna *(Compassion)*

All I have to medicate the insect bites that consume the entire lower part of my face is Chinese tiger balm, which burns and burns. My ears are scabbed, my neck beaded with welts. And the best benefit of being bald—I have mosquito bites ringing my scalp, pockets of pain breaking through the hard stubble of my curls. I've never seen so many stupid, creepy bugs in my life!

I never imagined that the vow not to kill would be so complicated, that I'd have to choreograph my smallest action so as to avoid inadvertently stepping on ants. I mean, we are living in the jungle! Unlike other precepts, not killing calls for constant awareness and an immense sense of personal responsibility.

Ways to Murder:
- *Not studying the path while walking*
- *Wearing shoes*
- *Breathing with mouth open*
- *Breathing through nose without a veil covering face*
- *Leaving glass of water uncovered*
- *Quick, brushing movements*

No matter how often I scrub the toilet, gnats drown in the shallow bowl, tiny black lines ticking off my sins like the days of a prison sentence. It makes sense to avoid killing in civilization where everyone is half-consciously swatting anything that gets in the way, but I'm tired of coaxing 10 ants out of my glass just to take a sip of water, of dribbling warning water around the toilet so that the gnats fly off and I can pee without committing sin, of feeling bugs crawl between my legs as I'm drifting off to sleep, of concentrating on pain, pain, pain while yet another creature is sucking my blood—the very moment I'm trying to cultivate compassion.

The first precept of Buddhism—to refrain from harming any living creature—was also the first law of my mother's household, the only offense to garner actual physical punishment. The specific rules of engagement, however, were complicated. As with Buddhism, lack of intention or awareness didn't matter. When my Aunt Ines handed me a salt shaker and directed me toward the mossy path mottled with early-morning slugs, and I trembled to discover that the blobs dissolved in a shower of salt, first foaming, then shriveling into phosphorescent ooze, I was expected to know that what I was doing was horribly cruel.

And I had known, to be honest—even without the expression on Mom's face—or at least suspected but had pushed this knowing into a corner, letting my fascination with color, transformation, danger take precedence, absolving myself from awareness and responsibility. My blindness was a temporary refusal to align action and intention, cause and effect. Where did I imagine the slugs had gone, after all?

Guilt-ridden once the killing was complete, the community of benign, spotted creatures reduced to smears of mustard, I got off on a technicality. I'd been obeying an adult's command: Kill.

The second time I have no such excuse.

The neighbor boy, David, and I are in the barn, the sun filtering through slats in the roof, forming thick, hazy columns of dust motes. We're swinging on a long, rough rope, lobbing ourselves into the bounce of hay. I feel the warm scratch against my face and arms and legs, inhale the musty odor of horses and old spaces.

We sink into the bales and discover a nest of newborn baby mice, smaller than my thumb, completely pink, covered with the softest white down. We can almost see through their translucent, veined ears. Eyes still closed, they squeal faintly for their mother. I've never seen anything so tiny in my entire life. They don't seem real.

Their papery ears and will-o'-the-wisp tails and waving claws are so miniature, so doll-like, that we're tempted to pull on them to see if they're really attached. We do, giving a gentle tug, and a single, crimson droplet of blood wells up where the ear had been. Horrified, we pull off the other ear, the tail, one arm and then another, the legs. Each yields to our trembling fingers so quickly, so easily that we're unable to stop.

I have no idea how many mice we do this to. Wherever I look, all I can see is that first, impossibly round, impossibly bright speck of blood.

The baby mice are now frightening—mewling little thumb-shaped bodies without definition. Tiny torsos and mouths scream for their missing limbs.

Terrified by what we've done, we drown them in the horse trough.

I don't remember what happened next or what made Mom decide to come all the way out to the barn to check on us, whether she figured out our crime or we confessed, trembling with chills, like the time I jumped from the rafters and came up howling, a rusty nail sticking through my boot, like the time the skittish mare stampeded and David got caught trying to slide under the wire fence, its jagged, black teeth laying open the soft flesh of his back in a 6-inch furrow.

For the first time since reaching "a reasoning age," I get spanked. The reality of Mom's hand against my flesh stuns me, but I can't really feel it, I'm already sobbing so.

Upekkha *(Equanimity & Calm)*

This evening head nun Roongdüan stresses the importance of developing compassion toward all creatures, especially dangerous ones. I wonder why. Sure, we free ourselves from crippling fear, but since when do the things we fear need our compassion?

Ever since her encounters with cobras on thudong, *she doesn't fear them. When she accidentally steps on a snake on the path, she says "KhƏƏ thôod." Excuse me.*

The conversation makes me nervous. So far every issue she's brought up in my evening lesson has been perfectly timed for use in meditation.

She compares training the mind through meditation to the desire to catch a fish. We wade into the paddy, up to our calves in mud, and search. At last we grasp what seems to be a fish, but upon withdrawing our hand, realize that it is a snake. What to do? Barehanded, we cannot kill the snake; stuck in the water, we cannot fling it away for fear that it will twist back and strike. So we whirl it around and around our head until it tires, then fling it away and run in the opposite direction.

Despite my mother's best intentions, I eventually learned to lie and to kill. When I was 6, we moved to my grandparents' farm in the semi-desert of southeastern Washington state, where Mummi waged a grim, daily battle against insects and dust. I was continually throwing back my covers, ready to spring into bed, to find a spider, hairy and angular, in the middle of my white sheets. Each time I screamed, indignant and aggrieved, while Mom tried to soothe me, saying, "It's only a house spider. It's not that big. Aren't you glad it eats mosquitoes and flies?"

No, I wasn't glad. My grandmother's child, I fantasized about knocking aside Mom's rocking chair and stomping her latest ward. I wouldn't even scrape the cracked body and green pulp off the bottom of my shoes. "Kill it!" I'd shriek, pointing to the intruder.

It was lying, however, that proved to be my true talent. I couldn't prevaricate about small, daily matters like receiving too much change, but I felt no compunction to honesty when it came to the big stuff. After all, I'd stared so intently at the TV during the snake documentary and been so mesmerized by the mutant, two-headed one, its dominant head dragging the minor one around like a spaced-out

Hindu deity, that I began to feel I'd really seen the snake. I'd been watching; I'd admitted its existence; I'd felt affinity; perhaps I did indeed see it.

My lies were crafted to reveal a greater truth than I believed the facts allowed. All my life I'd been told that my truth was not possible, from playground accusations that my white mother had adopted me, to my teachers' refusals to accept my writing skills. And so I gave myself authorial authority, my verbal creations the Tawny Taupe nail polish tanning the once-pink paper doll. I lied to hold shame at bay —Sure, I'd been born in a real hospital, not a home for unwed mothers. Sure, I'd seen my unknown father and siblings; I visited Nigeria all the time. Sure, I could speak our native tongue. There was indeed a place I belonged. My reality was closer to the truth. And a better reality was what I was after, if it took colorizing books and paper dolls or lying to get there.

Upekkha *(Equanimity & Calm)*

After this talk of dangerous creatures, I go inside my hut, turn on the light, and there as I had expected—though not quite this soon—is my test: A huge spider, glossy black, some 4 inches in diameter, hangs on the wall above my mat. I sink to the floor and try to calm down. What are the Buddhist answers to get me out of this moment? Awareness. I consider what a spider is, break it down into its components. Contemplation. I focus on the shiny black ball and eight, jointed legs. I consider how irrational my fear is. I breathe.

The spider remains. Ugly, mythic. Scotty, beam me the hell up! I want to flee, screaming. Not possible. I want to cry with the realization that from now on we might be roommates. Possible, though not recommended.

I close my eyes and manage a few ragged breaths. My cheeks quiver as I fight the urge to pop open my eyes and keep tabs on my visitor.

A loud thumping forces me to look up. The planks of the wall connecting to the bathroom contract in and out, one after the other, as if a heavy steel ball were being rolled across. The wood creaks and flares.

I jump up and grab the flashlight. Reaching the bathroom I throw open the door, flick on the torch, and stop short.

A muscular monitor lizard, its body a full foot long and some 3 inches thick, clings to the wall above my head. Squat, bowed legs center its weight; claws dig deep into the wooden planks. Chain-mail scales shimmer blue in the circle of light from the flashlight. In a single, fluid motion, its flat snake's head swivels a smooth 180 degrees toward me, the slit eyes rotating, focusing, locking.

I stumble back and switch off the flashlight. The Thai call monitor lizards thú-gàe *after the resonant, prehistoric rumble of their call. My breath sounds in the damp bathroom—short, wet, like a dripping faucet. My hands shake like a malaria victim's. I try to focus. I'm distracted by thoughts of the lizard's weight as it moved across the wall, all cold-blooded muscle and teeth, cousin to the dinosaur.*

The Thai say that thú-gàe *lock their jaws during attack and nothing short of burning them off will loosen their grip. I can just see myself—victim of the first precept not to kill—with the damn thing latched to my forehead for the rest of my life!*

I take a deep breath and two quavering steps forward, hoping to get the lizard used to me. Immediately its tail shoots up, an 8-inch exclamation. The air thickens between us. Is this a warning, a prelude to attack? How to interpret the actions of a reptile? How to anticipate them? Will it attack out of malice or only if provoked? What constitutes provocation? Is a temple-dwelling reptile concerned with the acquisition of merit?

After a few minutes, I concede defeat. I have no idea what to do, and the monitor is giving no clues. I slide by the mass of blue steel, its tail still aloft, and return to my hut, disheartened.

I often find myself wondering why we have to be braver than other women. Isn't it enough that we're different?

When at the age of 22 I moved into the Thai forest, shaved my head and eyebrows, donned white robes, and ordained, I agreed to live by 10 precepts and numerous behavioral codes. When I left the temple, I exchanged my nun vows for the five basic precepts to which Buddhist citizens adhere: to refrain from killing, stealing, sexual offense, lying, and consuming intoxicants. Even as I took the five citizen precepts, I knew I was lying. Taking them was only a transitional measure to lessen my anxiety at disrobing. I knew that for me there was no Middle Path. I was either ordained or not. Of the spirit or of the flesh.

I justified my five lies easily. Since the purpose of the precepts is to enhance the practice of mindfulness, thereby liberating oneself from the cycle of bad karma and rebirth, and not to assign sin, there was no reason not to return to alcohol and sex. And I wasn't going to give up lying, my natural talent. There was no way, however, to justify killing.

In the 13 years since disrobing, I've wondered about my determination not to break the first precept. I certainly don't adhere to the letter of the law—I wear shoes and leather; I drive a car; I eat meat; I breathe with impunity—but I won't raise my hand with the intention to destroy life. It's a matter not of virtue but dread.

And so the precept that proved hardest to follow as a nun is the only one I still keep. Not because it directly impacts the welfare of others but because it presents a continual challenge, reminding me what is possible, 13 years out of the temple, 17 years out of my mother's house.

Metta *(Love & Goodwill)*

We hunker down to wait out monsoon season. No one can leave the temple. Head nun Roongdüan explains it's because so many creatures emerge during the rains that it would be virtually impossible to move without killing. According to my history text, however, wandering mendicants gathered together at rain retreats long before Buddhism's spread because the rains made it difficult to travel. Our temple population swells with the stream.

The rains bring insects. A praying mantis, spiders the size of fists, bug larvae that dive-bomb my candle and writhe on the mat, still smoking. I erect a makeshift candle cover from an empty saline bottle to protect them from accidental suicide.

The temple is warmer, lusher, greener. I meditate with my door open to night, my hut lit by a single flame. Head nun Roongdüan's face glows in the flicker of her own candle. "Go back to meditating," she whispers. "I brought you juice. Do you have enough candles? Any problems?"

She beams confidence in me, so I don't tell her that I've been crying. That I'm so very, very lonely. That I opened my eyes while meditating in the cave and discovered that the soft noises I've been hearing as the air swirls through the darkness are in fact rats. As soon as the sun goes down, they emerge in packs from the recesses of the cave. I opened my eyes to see them swarming over the figure of the Buddha, his eyes downcast in a golden, smiling face.

"No problems, right?" she prompts.

Right. I am filled with love.

I finally feel like a nun and not someone pretending to move slowly, dog-paddling in air to kill time. When a breeze blows the gauze at the door back and I catch a glimpse of another nun—a silent figure in white—I am reminded of something mysterious, not quite human or ordinary. I feel light, indistinct, something people can't quite look at or see. The Naga.

Faith Adiele *won the Millenium Award from Creative Nonfiction for this essay. She is the daughter of a Scandinavian-American mother and Nigerian father, was raised in the Pacific Northwest, and has lived in Southeast Asia and West Africa. Her nonfiction has appeared in Ms. Magazine, Transition, Ploughshares, Fourth Genre and numerous anthologies. Her honors include designation as a PEN New England Emerging Writer, the Willard R. Espy Award in Nonfiction, the Zora Neale Hurston/Richard Wright Award in Fiction, and fellowships from Yaddo, the MacDowell Colony and the Banff Center for the Arts. She lives in Iowa City.*

The Brown Study

Richard Rodriguez

Or, as a brown man, I think.

But do we really think that color colors thought? Sherlock Holmes occasionally retired to a "brown study"—a kind of moribund funk; I used to imagine a room with brown wallpaper. I think, too, of the process—the plunger method—by which coffee sometimes is brewed. The grounds commingle with water for a time and then are pressed to the bottom of the carafe by a disk or plunger. The liquid, cleared of sediment, is nevertheless colored, substantially coffee. (And *coffee-colored* has come to mean coffee-and-cream-colored; and coffee with the admixture of cream used to be called *blond*. And vanilla has come to mean white, bland, even though vanilla extract, to the amazement of children, is brown as iodine, and *vanilla-colored*, as in Edith Sitwell's "where vanilla-coloured ladies ride," refers to Manila and to brown skin.) In the case of brown thought, though, I suppose experience becomes the pigment, the grounds, the mise-en-scène, the medium of refraction, the speed of passage of otherwise pure thought.

In a florescent-lit jury room attached to a superior court in San Francisco, two jurors were unconvinced and unmoving. I was unconvinced because of the gold tooth two bank tellers had noticed. The other juror was a man late in his 20s—rather preppy, I thought on first meeting—who prefaced his remarks with, "As a black man, I think..."

I have wondered, ever since, if that were possible. If I do have brown thoughts.

Not brown enough. I was once taken to task—rather, I was made an example of—by that woman from the Threepenny Review as the sort of writer, the callow, who parades his education. I use literary allusion as a way of showing off, proof that I have mastered a white idiom, whereas the true threepenny intellectual assumes everybody knows everything, or doesn't, or can't, or shouldn't, or needn't, and there you are. Which makes me a sort of monkey-do.

Well, you see, I thought I was supposed to. I wasn't decorating my remarks. Was I too eager to join the conversation? It's only now I realize there is no conversation. Allusion is bounded by Spell Check.

After such a long education, most perceptions authentically "remind." And I'm not the only one. The orb Victoria held in her hand has passed to her brown children who, like Christchildren in old paintings, toy with the world a bit, and then, when no one is looking, pop it into their mouths. The only person I know for whom the novels of Trollope are urgent lives in India.

It is interesting, too, to wonder whether what is white about my thought is impersonation, minstrelsy. Is allusion inauthentic, Ms. Interlocutor, when it comes from a brown sensibility? My eyes are brown. *Cheeks of tan?*

Most bookstores have replaced disciplinary categories with racial identification, or sexual. In either case I must be shelved Brown. The most important theme of my writing now is impurity. My mestizo boast: As a queer, Catholic, Indian Spaniard at home in a temperate, Chinese city in a fading, blond state in a post-Protestant nation, I live up to my 16th-century birth.

The future is brown, is my thesis—is as brown as the tarnished past. Brown may be as refreshing as green. We shall see. L.A., unreal city, is brown already, though it wasn't the other day I was there—it was rain-rinsed and as bright as a dark age. But on many days, the air turns fuscous from the scent glands of planes and from Lexus musk. The pavements, the palisades—all that jungly stuff one sees in the distance—are as brown as an oxidized print of a movie—brown as old Roman gardens or pennies in a fountain, brown as gurgled root beer, tobacco, monkey fur, catarrh.

We are accustomed, too, to thinking of antiquity as brown, browning. Darkening, as memory darkens, as the Dark Ages were dark. They weren't, of course; they were highly painted and rain-rinsed. We just don't remember clearly. I seem to remember the ceiling, how dark it was. How tall it seemed. The kitchen ceiling. And how frail we are! What used to be there? A shoe store? A newsstand? I seem to remember it, right about here…a red spine, wasn't it? Have I felt that before? Or is this cancer?

At last, the white thought, the albin pincer—pain—an incipient absence, like a puddle of milk or the Milky Way. *The glacier knocks in the cupboard.* Why is cancer the white ghost? Why are ghosts white? And what year was that? Which play? Well, obviously it's Shakespeare. "Lear"? "Cymbeline"? *Golden lads and girls all must…*Death is black. Coffee may be black, but black is not descriptive of coffee. Coffee is not descriptive of death. Can one's life be brown? My eyes are brown, but my life? Youth is green, and optimism; Gatsby believed in the green light.

Whereas there is brown at work in all the works of man. By the 18th century, the majority of Mexico was mestizo, neither "pure" Indian nor "pure" Spaniard—brown. Time's passage is brown. Decomposition. Maggots. Foxing—the bookman's term—reddish brown, reynard. Manuscripts, however jewel-like, from Dark Ages, will darken. Venice will darken. Celluloid darkens, as if the lamp of the projector were insufficient sun. College blue books. Fugitive colors. My parents!

If we wish to antique an image, to make memory of it, we print it in sepia tone—sepia, an extract from the occluding ink of the octopus, of the cuttlefish, now an agent for kitsch. Whereas the colors, the iridescent Blakes at the Tate, are housed now in perpetual gloom, lest colors be lifted from the page by the cutpurse sun. The Kodachrome prints in your closet—those high-skied and hopeful summer days—are dimming their lights, and the skies are lowering. Would we be astounded by the quality of light in 1922?

> *Unreal City*
> *Under the brown fog of a winter dawn,*
> *A crowd flowed over London Bridge, so many,*
> *I had not thought death had undone so many.*

The prince had always liked his London, when it had come to him. And it had come to him that morning with a punctual, unembarrassed rap at the door, a lamp switched on in the sitting room, a trolley forced over the threshold, chiming its cups and its spoons. The valet, second floor, in alto, Hindu Cockney—and with a startled professionalism (I am browner than he)—proposed to draw back the drapes, brown, thick as theater curtains.

Outside the hotel, several floors down, a crowd of blue- and green-haired teen-agers kept a dawn vigil for a glimpse of their Faerie Queene. Indeed, as the valet fussed with the curtain, they recommenced their chant of "Mah-don-ahh. Mah-don-ahh."

Madonna was in town and staying at this hotel. All day and all night, the approach or departure of any limousine elicited the tribute.

Mah-don-ahh was in town making a film about Eva Peron (both women familiar with the uses of peroxide. Not such a bad thing to know in the great, brown world, Oi, mate?).

I was in London because my book had just come out there. My book about Mexico. Not a weight on most British minds.

Did I ever tell you about my production of "The Tempest"? I had been at the theater the previous evening. Not "The Tempest" but the new Stoppard, and I watched with keener interest as the Asian in front of me leaned over to mouth little babas into the be-ringed ear of his Cockney hire. One such confidence actually formed a bubble. Which in turn reminded me of my production of "The Tempest." (South Sea Bubble.) I would cast Maggie Smith as Miranda—wasted cheeks and bugging eyes—a buoyant Miss Haversham, sole valedictorian of her papa's creepy seminary. Caliban would be Johnny Depp. No fish scales, no seaweed, no webbed fingers, no claws, no vaudeville. No clothes. Does anybody know what I'm talking about? Ah, me. I am alone in my brown study. I can say anything I like. Nobody listens.

Will there be anything else, sir?

No, nothing else, thank you.

Brown people know there is nothing in the world—no recipe, no water, no city, no motive, no lace, no locution, no candle, no corpse that does not—I was going to say descend—that does not become brown. Brown might, as well, be making.

My little Caliban book, as I say, bound in iguana hide, was about Mexico. With two newspapers under my arm, and balancing a cup of coffee, I went back to my bed. I found the Book Section; I found the review. I knew it! I read first the reviewer's bio: a gay, Colombian writer living in London.

What the book editor had done—dumb London book editor of the *Observer* had done, as Kansas City does and Manhattan does—is find my double, or the closest he could find, in greater London. It's a kind of doppelgänger theory of literary criticism and it's dishearteningly fashionable among the liberal-hearted. In our age of "diversity," the good and the liberal organize diversity. Find a rhyme for orange. If one is singular or outlandish, by this theorem, one can't be reviewed at all. Worse than that, if one is unlike, one will not be published. Publishers look for the next, rather than the first, which was accident. But the Observer wasn't even within bow-range. Their gay gaucho was clueless.

The liberal-hearted who run the newspapers and the university English departments and organize the bookstores have turned literature into well-meaning sociology. Thus do I get invited by the editor at some magazine to review your gay translation of a Colombian who has written a magical-realist novel. Trust me, there has been little magical realism in my life since my first trip to Disneyland.

That warm, winter night in Tucson. My reading was scheduled for the 6:30 slot by the University of Arizona. A few hundred people showed up—old more than young, mostly brown. I liked my "them," in any case, for coming to listen, postponing their dinners. In the middle of a paragraph, a young man stood to gather his papers, then retreated up the aisle, pushed open the door at the back of the auditorium. In the trapezoid of lobby light thus revealed, I could see a crowd was forming for the 8 o'clock reading—a lesbian poet. Then the door closed, silently sealing the present. I continued reading but wondered to myself, Why couldn't I get the lesbians for an evening? And the lesbian poet serenade my Mexican-American audience? Wouldn't that be truer to the point of literature?

Well, what's the difference? I do not see myself as a writer in the world's eye, much less a white writer, much less a Hispanic writer, much less "a writer" in the 92nd Street Y sense. I'd rather be Madonna. Really, I would.

The Frankfurt Book Fair has recently been overrun with Koreans and Indians who write in English (the best English novelist in the world is not British at all but a Mahogany who lives in snowy Toronto and writes of Bombay). Inevitably, the pale conclusion is that brown writers move "between" cultures. I resist *between*, prefer *among* or *because of*. You keep the handicap. After all, it has taken several degrees of contusion to create a jaundice as pervasive as mine. It has taken a lifetime of compromises, the thinning of hair, the removal last year of a lesion from my scalp, the assurance of loneliness, the difficulty of prayer, an amused knowledge of five-star hotels—and death—and a persistence of childish embarrassments and evermore prosaic Roman Catholic hymns, to entertain a truly off-white thought. Here comes one now. *Un marron!*

No, I guess not. There's a certain amount of "So what?" that comes with middle age. But is that brown thought?

Thus did literary ambition shrivel in my heart, in a brown room in a creamy hotel in London, constructed as a 19th-century hospital and recently renovated to resemble a Victorian hotel that never existed except in the minds of a Hispanic author from California and a blond movie star from New Jersey.

Eve's apple, or what was left of it, quickly browned.

"Christ! A white doorway!" was Bukowski's recollection of having taken a bite on the apple. When Eve looked again, she saw a brown crust had formed over the part where she had eaten and invited Adam's lip. It was then she threw the thing away from her. Thenceforward (the first Thenceforward), Brown informed everything she touched.

Don't touch! Touch will brown the rose and the Acropolis, will spoil the butterfly's wing. (Creation mocks us with incipient brown.) The call of nature is brown, even in five-star hotels. The mud we make reminds us that we are: *In the sweat of thy face shalt thou eat bread, till thou return into the ground; for out of it wast thou taken...*

Toil is brown. Bruegel's peasants are brown, I remember noting in a Vienna museum.

In his book "Abroad," Paul Fussell reminds us how, early in the 20th century, the relative ease of modern travel and boredom allowed moneyed Americans and Europeans to extrude the traditional meaning of the laborer's brown and to make of it a glove of leisure. What the moon had been for early 19th-century romantics, the sun became for bored 20th-century romantics. The brown desired by well-to-do Europeans was a new cure altogether: tan.

There is another fashionable brown. An untouchable brown. Certain shrewd, ancient cities have evolved an aesthetic of decay, making the best of necessity. Decrepitude can seem to ennoble whomever or whatever chic is placed in proximity—Anita Ekberg, Naomi Campbell. The tanned generation, aka the Lost Generation, gamboled through the ruins of the Belle Époque. The *cardinali* of post-war drug culture—Paul Bowles, William Burroughs—found heaven in North Africa, mansions white. It's a Catholic idea, actually—that the material world is redeemed; that time is continuous; that one can somehow be redeemed by the faith of an earlier age or a poorer class if one lives within its shadow or its arrondissement, breathes its sigh. And lately fashion photographers, bored with Rome or the Acropolis, have ventured further afield for the frisson of syncretism. Why not Calcutta? Why not the slums of Rio? Cairo? Mexico City? The attempt is for an unearned, casual brush with awe by enlisting untouchable extras. And if the model can be seen to move with idiot stridency through tragedy, then the model is invincible. Luxury is portrayed as protective. Or protected. Austere, somehow—"spiritual." Irony posing as asceticism or as worldly wise.

One of the properties of awe is untouchability. *Silènzio*, the recorded voice booms through the Sistine Chapel at five- or 10-minute intervals. *Do not speak. Do not touch.* Even resurrected Christ—the white doorway himself—backed away from Mary Magdalene's dirty fingernails. Don't touch! I would have expected a Roman Catholic understanding of time to accommodate centuries of gaping mouths, respiration, prayer, burnt offerings—and reticence—offering the exemplum of a clouded ceiling to 20th-century pilgrims. After all, we live in time. Our glimpse of the Eternal must be occluded by veils of time, of breath, of human understanding.

The human imagination has recently sustained a reversal.

One would have expected the pope, as the pre-eminent upholder of the natural order, to have expressed reservations about the cleaning of the Sistine ceiling. The pope, however, in a curiously puritanical moment, gave his blessing to a curator's blasphemy, which was underwritten by the Japanese fetish for the cleaning of history. The blasphemy was to imagine that restoring the ceiling might restore the Vatican's luster. The blasphemy was to imagine that time might be reversed. The blasphemy was to believe that time should be reversed.

The human imagination has recently sustained a reversal. We have cleaned the ceiling. Michelangelo's "Creation" and "Judgment," the first and the last and the pride of centuries—a vault over the imagination of the world—have been cleaned, have been restored, unhallowed, changed and called "original," though no one has any idea what that might mean. (What was the light of day in 1540?) Nile greens and rose-petal pinks, tangier oranges and the martyred saints—what supernal beaver-shots. Well, we want them preserved, of course we do. And we are keen to see them as *they*, the dead, saw them, as Michelangelo painted them. The very Tree of Knowledge has been restored, each leaf rinsed and all the fruit polished, the fruit and the sin re-polished. Having seen, we also want them back the way they were.

We want what Eve wanted…*Just curious.*

We had become accustomed to an averted eye, to seeing darkly, as old men see. It required many thousands of Q-Tips, many thousands of gallons of distilled water, which is to say, merely a couple of years, to wipe away the veil of tears, the glue from awakened eyes, to see born-again Adam touched by the less complicated hand of God. Now our distance from the representations, both alpha and omega, has been removed. And with it all credibility.

Blind John Milton—*brown all!*—dictating "Paradise Lost" to his aggrieved daughter in the dark, understood that what changes after Adam's sin is not creation but our human relationship to creation. (We cannot be content, even on a warm, winter day in L.A., but we must always carp about a white Christmas.)

Maybe Milton, in this sense, in his preoccupation with the Fall, was more an ancient, swarthy Catholic than a true, ready Protestant. (Protestantism was also an attempt to clean the ceiling.) Those famous religious refugees from Restoration England were (like Milton) Puritans who believed they had entered a green time and were elected by God to be new Adams, new Eves (as old John Milton could not, with the scabs of Europe grown over his eyes, and painted tropes of angels plaguing his memory—*brown all, brown all*).

Let us speak of desire as green. In the Roman church, green is the color of Ordinary Time, a prosaic pathway. For American Puritans, green was extraordinary. They supposed themselves re-made by their perilous journey to a new world they were determined to call green, proclaiming by that term their own refreshment. They had entered a garden ungardened and felt themselves free of history, free to re-enact the drama of creation.

Green became the founding flag of America; and so it would remain for generations of puritans to come, whatever our religion or lack. American optimism—our sense of ourselves as decent, naive, primary people (compared to those violet, cynical races); our sense of ourselves as young, our sap rising, our salad days always before us, our belief that the eastern shore the Europeans "discovered" and the fruited plain beyond were, after all, "virgin"—all this would follow from an original belief in the efficacy of green.

Thus did the Dutch sailors in F. Scott Fitzgerald's "Great Gatsby" spy the sheer cleft of an approaching "fresh green breast." That same green breast is today the jaded tip of Long Island, summer home to New Amsterdam investment bankers and other rewarded visionaries who do not resemble their portraits. And the tragic hustler's ghost:

> *Gatsby believed in the green light, the orgiastic future that year by year recedes before us. It eluded us then, but that's no matter—tomorrow we will run faster, stretch out our arms farther...And one fine morning...*

We—I write in the early months of the 21st century—we are now persuaded by Marxist literary critics to goddamn any green light, to hack away at any green motif. Someone off-stage has suffered, and no good can come of it. We are a college of victims, we post-moderns; we are more disposed to notice Fitzgerald's Dutch sailors were not alone upon the landscape (we easily pick out chameleon Indians hidden among the green tracery) than we are to wonder at the expanding, original iris: How the Indians must have marveled at those flaxen-haired Dutchmen.

Well, most likely the Indians were too terrified to morphologize or eroticize on the spot. *What happens next?* Watch, as the Indians did watch—with darker dread and puzzlement—what cargo these pale sailors unloaded. From below deck emerged Africa in chains, the sun in thrall to the moon.

Thus, perceiving Europeans having only just arrived, the Indians already saw. Indians saw Original Sin. The dark ceiling. The stain spreading like oil spill. Rumor, too, must have spread like wildfire across the Americas—making green impossible from that moment except as camouflage or tea.

Forgetting for the moment the journeys of others and the lateness of the hour, considering only the founding triad of our clandestine exhibit—Indian, European, African—we see (as well as the Founding Sin) the generation of the erotic motif of America. A brown complexity—complexity of narrative and of desire—can be foretold from the moment Dutch sailors and African slaves meet within the Indian eye.

I think I probably do. (Have brown thoughts.)

Richard Rodriguez *is an editor at Pacific News Service and a contributor to Harper's Magazine, U.S. News & World Report and the Sunday opinion section of the Los Angeles Times. His work appears in the New York Times, Wall Street Journal, American Scholar, Time, Mother Jones, New Republic and other publications. His books include "Hunger of Memory and Days of Obligation: An Argument With My Mexican Father." He also has written two BBC documentaries. Rodriguez received the Peabody Award in 1997 for his "NewsHour" essays on American life. Other awards include the Frankel Medal from the National Endowment for the Humanities and the International Journalism Award from the World Affairs Council of California. He lives in San Francisco.*

Blindsided

Julia Copeland

*L*ast week I discovered I was black.

You might think that is something you can't just discover in middle age, but stranger things—even similar things (Madeleine Albright finding out about her Jewish heritage)—have happened. In my case some old documents came to light—a relative was doing some sleuthing in genealogy and made this stunning find. I had no reason to doubt the news, just as I had no reason to suspect it before it became news. Does this seem impossible to you, to be black and not know it? To be thus—as I just put it, choosing a word that now seems to carry racist overtones—*stunned*? I too might have thought so before my cousin's announcement. But of course it's not impossible. In fact it must be the case for hundreds, thousands of Americans, probably more, not to mention numbers of others the world over. What, after all, does it mean to *pass*? To pass is to move from one census box to another. It's a move that is, in the absence of genetic reminders, quite simple and quite final. Once the physical signs have been erased, who is to keep the purely theoretical connections alive? Forgetting is, arguably, a choice. But it is a choice that has often been made.

I have been white for almost 50 years. Or should I say *had* been white? What exactly must that change of tense mean?

I'll tell you one thing: For the past week it's meant a wildly increased self-consciousness and an increased curiosity. It's not just that I'm checking the moons of my fingernails, as people used to do in 19th-century America, assured by experts on race that the fingernails were a dead giveaway, that anyone could tell just by looking at those telltale moons (blue moons, some said) that you were black under your white skin. But I am reconsidering a bit. I'm thinking for example of a couple of aunts with their frizzy perms in the 1950s. I try to bring the memory-films into closeup. Was there anything I should have noticed about these aunts? Was there any chance those weren't perms at all? Suddenly any familial flatness of nose or thickness of lip takes on new significance. And what about those who used to tan easily, as people always said? Anything there?

Were there hidden births, dark children shunted off to adoption agencies? I have a hazily dramatic picture of the world of unbreachable social walls, a world of stealth and tragedy, as portrayed in movies and fiction from the '30s through the '70s. More recent history seems recorded in garish Technicolor, with an emphasis on colorblindness that seems paradoxically to exaggerate color difference while seeking to deny it.

I myself was colorblind till a few days ago.

The Next Morning

The next morning I was looking in the mirror at that mole I've hated since it appeared a few years ago on my temple. Last week it was an annoyance; this week it's something else. Melanin, I think, as I comb my hair to cover it. Melanin. Is that the most important ingredient? I'm thinking disconnectedly of the "Black Like Me" author, John Howard Griffin, who endured chemical treatments to darken his skin and then traveled—under cover of darkness, one might say—through the '50s South. He died of it, so the story goes, died of the treatment through which he achieved his racial crossover.

That next morning I was looking in the mirror, and such a host of new thoughts crashed in on me that I seemed actually to be another person. I looked the same, but I was carrying some other person's baggage. Toting, perhaps I mean. I touched my face and considered these strange new thoughts. Then I took a pencil and began writing. I wrote:

> There is only one great subject in America, and that is race. And the central strangeness of the subject is that, despite the fact that the word race now seems to many of us to be included in the word America—in fact it is included in the word America ("I am race," declares one anagram)— it's a subject that seems, in discussions of America, in our thinking about the concept of America, brand new. Because America in my childhood

meant white America. America meant "us," with a separate, struggling "them" whose troubles we watched on television.

And I wrote:

There is also only one racial color duo in America, only one that counts: black and white. Other concerns, the questions of various shades of brown, can't come anywhere near that central one in importance.

Others, it turned out, had been there before me. "There are only two qualities in the United States racial pattern: white and black," wrote Carl Degler in 1971. "A person is one or the other: There is no intermediate position." And much earlier—in 1893—James Bryce observed, "In Latin America whoever is not black is white; in Teutonic America whoever is not white is black."

But that next morning I hadn't started consulting books yet. I was still thinking those first, unfamiliar thoughts. I looked up from my writing and thought, *I should call Tess and tell her the news.* And then I thought, *Good heavens, you can't just call up the only black person you ever counted as a friend, because that's how it has been—for whatever reason, you've had only one black friend (visibly black, I must now amend) to speak of—you can't just call up Tess, who anyway has been only distantly connected in the past 15 years since both of you moved away from the city where your friendship flourished. You can't just call up a black friend out of the blue (or out of the blue moon) to happen to mention this in—as it were—passing. What is that news supposed to mean to her? That she should shout out for joy? That we should suddenly become as close as sisters? What words would I even use?*

Hyphenation

It's not like Godfrey Cambridge in "Watermelon Man" or Keenan Wynn in "Finian's Rainbow." Those guys woke up black. One day they were white; the next day they were anything but. The contrast was funny and made for trenchant social commentary. But I don't look any different. When I wake up, I am exactly the same, with the added element of memory: Now I have, in some sense, if only provisionally and on my cousin's say-so, a racial heritage.

I didn't before. I was never a hyphenated American of any kind. I didn't even look any particular way—neither particularly light nor particularly dark. People had assumed me to be French, English, Scottish, Scandinavian or Canadian, Jewish on occasion, but never black. (Note the confusion of categories—nationality, religion, "race" —which is which?). I blended into the background, invisible. Ellison's Man was only metaphorically Invisible—he had, like any black-skinned person in a majority-white society, distinct physical visibility. I have none of that. I was used to my default racelessness. I had always just assumed that my family's nebulous history was the result of inevitable melting-pot conglomeration. And it was—just more dramatically so, more significantly so than I could have guessed.

Photo

Looking through today's newspaper, seeing a photograph in an article about African-American voters protesting the Bush election, I'm noticing the face of the young boy in the foreground of the shot. His features are even and handsome. His skin could be any color—in this rendition it's a light gray, very light. I find him good-looking, but I'm now asking myself whether by *good-looking* I mean *white-looking*, and I think I probably do to some extent. And I'm also thinking of him as halfway related to me, because he's identified as African-American, and now I have been, too. But before—before last week—would I have identified him as related to me on the basis of the mixed-race look of his face, the obvious Caucasian (do we still use that term?) influence? I don't think so. And that's a curious thing, is it not?

More Photos

I did not call my erstwhile friend Tess. But I thought about her a lot. I remembered for example how I had been amazed by a group of family photographs she kept—beautifully arranged, artfully arranged —in her house on a table also piled with candles and flowers, like a shrine. I remembered my exact thoughts when looking at that group of photos: *These people are not black.* When you live as I had lived, sheltered in white, middle-class America, you do not generally devote much thought to fine gradations of blackness. You have your knee-jerk liberal reactions, perhaps, inherited from your parents, if you are lucky. You have flaunted as a schoolchild your equal-housing button stabbed through the cover of your history notebook. You smile at everyone equally but maybe a little more at those with dark skin. You mouth the platitudes: We are all brothers under the skin; no one should be discriminated against on the basis of the color of his skin. But you do not generally come up against the tough questions: What is skin color? How does it relate to life in this world? What does it mean to those whose skin is colored? How much color is "colored"?

A Single Drop

The United States is the only country in the world in which a white woman can give birth to a black baby but a black woman cannot give birth to a white baby.

In the late 1800s, in a reaction to the 14th and 15th amendments to the Constitution (guaranteeing black males the right to vote and ensuring that this right could not be taken away), the United States Supreme Court itself passed laws that held, as Albion Tourgée put it in 1896, that "a single drop of African blood is sufficient to color a whole ocean of Caucasian whiteness"—thus incorporating the unofficial "one-drop rule" into the rule of law.

F. James Davis explains:

To be considered black in the United States, not even half of one's ancestry must be African black. But will one-fourth do, or one-eighth, or less? The nation's answer to the question "Who is black?" has long been that a black is any person with any known African black ancestry. This definition reflects the long experience with slavery and later with Jim Crow segregation. In the South it became known as the "one-drop rule," meaning that a single drop of "black blood" makes a person a black. It is also known as the "one black ancestor rule"; some courts have called it the "traceable amount rule"; and anthropologists call it the "hypo-descent rule," meaning that racially mixed persons are assigned the status of the subordinate group.

All this rule-making presupposed that there was in fact such a thing as "black blood," that you could tell which drop was African. And of course now that we have sophisticated techniques for analyzing blood, we know that you can't. We know it when scientists explain it to us, telling us that "the extent of genic differentiation between human races is not always correlated with the degree of morphological differentiation," by which they mean that those who look like each other superficially may actually have less genetic material in common than those who do not. So we know that "race" is a construct, a handy fiction, an invention. We know, and yet we don't really know at all. Melanin confuses us. Skin and blood are terms forever twined, emptied or pumped full of meaning at the whim of whatever dark heart may be controlling the surge. Skin seems to reveal blood—can even literally do so, an observation Charles Chesnutt used in conjuring, in an 1898 story, the "Blue Vein Society," eligibility for which rested on being white enough to show blue veins through one's skin. Chesnutt was spoofing, but the beliefs he condemned were anything but a joke.

I suppose in the 19th century the question was more immediate, the opportunities for irony more pronounced. Mark Twain, in his 1894 novel, "Pudd'nhead Wilson," which involves the switching of two babies at birth—one allegedly white, the other allegedly black—writes of the mother of one of the boys:

> *To all intents and purposes Roxy was as white as anybody, but the one-sixteenth of her which was black out-voted the other fifteen parts and made her a negro. She was a slave, and salable as such. Her child was thirty-one parts white, and he, too, was a slave, and by a fiction of law and custom a negro.*

"Fiction of law and custom" is a strong statement and still thought-provoking after all these years, but Twain presses his analysis further, telling us that even someone who didn't know the two babes could tell them apart, despite their identical "blue eyes and flaxen curls," *by their clothes*:

> *for the white babe wore ruffled soft muslin and a coral necklace, while the other wore merely a coarse tow-linen shirt which barely reached his knees, and no jewelry.*

But few white Americans were pressing the nature/nurture question Twain here exposed. And law, which creates a fiction quite as solid as reality, continued to define and separate the "races" for another century. States had their own definitions, placed on the books at regular intervals. Notably explicit is Virginia's 1924 Act to Preserve Racial Integrity, which declared:

> *It shall be unlawful for any white person in this state to marry any save a white person, or a person with no other admixture of blood than white and American Indian. For the purpose of this act, the term "white person" shall apply only to the person who has no trace whatsoever of any blood other than Caucasian; but persons who have one-sixteenth or less of the blood of the American Indian and have no other non-caucasic blood shall be deemed to be white.*

Amazingly the United States is still ridding itself of these galls, picking them out of the hairy language of its legal system like stubborn burrs. Bans on interracial marriage were still being deleted from state constitutions as late as 1987.

?-cide

Part of the fear embedded in the series of statutes defining and outlawing miscegenation is this: the fear of obliteration. Certainly "passing" has been viewed as genocide—that really is the nature of the betrayal. It is an act of extermination, the rejection of one racial story in favor of another. But of course genocide is possible only when there is a commonly recognized and predefined *gens*, some agreed-upon idea of race. The reason miscegenation has been so feared historically is that it necessarily dismantles the concept of *gens*, blurs the lines meant to contain color. Miscegenation forces the erasure of boundaries, renders the old diagrams—with their conspicuously non-intersecting circles—obsolete, throws the whole notion of measurement into question. How can we know, without boundaries and definitions, who is to be hated, who is to be feared, who, exactly, is the enemy?

It's Everywhere

It's everywhere, this urge, this need to draw fine distinctions, make absurd rules, because otherwise how can you tell? How can you know for sure? And for some reason, long after slavery, long after installation of the insidiously misnamed "colorblindness," it's still urgently important *to know for sure*. It's still important to classify humans according to what has been, by a fiction of law and custom, called *race*. But what, whatever, is meant by that term? Even listening to the radio—"All Things Considered," mind you, not AM shock-talk—I find myself reacting with discomfort to a report that "blacks tend to" have this or that medical problem, or "African-Americans show" this or that physical propensity. Who are they talking about? "Them"? Me? I worry about this continued application of the "scientific method," which method, after all, brought us racial categories—with their retinue of now-discredited but still uneradicated notions about superior and inferior natural endowments—in the first place.

Once, before I'd ever imagined my cousin's discovery, I made an accidental experiment. A young woman functionary stopped me when I'd failed to check the race box on a form. I said I didn't believe in checking that box, but she said it was legally required. (Is that possible?) Anyway I refused. I walked away, leaving the form on her desk, and she called to my back, "I'm putting down White."

Really that's what it amounts to, isn't it? What you see is what you get? Race, unless you speak up, unless you make a claim, is entirely in the eye of the beholder.

Watermelon Woman

I'm not suddenly bilingual, like Barbara Billingsly, famous as the mother in "Leave It to Beaver," who in the movie "Airplane" played a white-haired lady fluent in jive. That was terrifically funny, the dignified WASP lady with her impeccable lineage in the whitest-of-white '50s television sitcoms, fluently speaking and easily translating (and of course being needed to translate) the incomprehensible mumbo-jumbo spoken by two dark-skinned basketball players.

Even Steve Martin's amusing and liberally motivated turnaround in "The Jerk," in which he plays a white guy who'd been adopted by a black family, is disturbing. Whether it reinforces or brilliantly critiques ingrained racialist assumptions, it nonetheless depends for its humor on the usual backward construction. Though we laugh when Martin reverses the direction of the joke—his character is atrociously, humiliatingly white, lacking, apparently genetically, any sense of rhythm or cool—we may feel coerced into unwilling collaboration, mocking but not rejecting the nature-instead-of-nurture hypothesis on which American racism has long depended.

You can appreciate the strangeness of the construct more when you are, even nominally, inside it. Watermelon, fried chicken, rap, basketball, dancing—did I ever think much about those things before? Why do I suddenly notice them? Where did all this meaning come from?

Like one of Twain's two flaxen-haired babies (the one dressed in ruffles and jewelry, the one who was, it turned out, the son of the slave Roxy), I have no experience being black.

More to the point, I have no training. And that's apparently what it would take. Race, in my newly adjusted view, appears to be this: 99 percent eye-of-the-beholder and 99 percent nurture. My math abilities were never very good. Now I suppose they reflect a racial deficiency as predicted by the bell curve.

Side Effect

It's been only a week. I'm sure I'll get used to this new tinge in my thinking. I can't see any difference, and of course no one has noticed —how could anyone?—but I'm oddly aware of one thing: not blackness, but whiteness. It's something I took for granted all my life —I lived in it, breathed in it, cloaked my assumptions in it. But what was it? It's as if there had been no such concept before. In any case it wasn't something that required attention. My understanding of whiteness was so absolute that I had no occasion to question the matter.

Now I do.

Julia Copeland's stories and essays have appeared in various publications, among them News From the Republic of Letters, the Louisville Review, the New Quarterly and the Writer's Chronicle. Now a Midwestern housewife and mother in Indiana, she was for many years a professional violinist.

Iguana Don

Patricia Frisella

A pea-green iguana cloaks the neck of a thin man dressed in chains and leather, striding along the train tracks. The iguana's golden eyes stare over one shoulder; its thick tail twitches over the other. I have seen this man before, but with a rifle, and a baby bundled in fuzzy blankets, over his shoulders. I worry about the man on the tracks. Trains, like bullets, arrive ahead of their sound. I wonder if he can feel vibrations through his heavy boots and why he does not use sidewalks.

It is not normal to see a man walking down train tracks with either an iguana or a baby. I wonder if this man, his iguana, baby and gun are homeless. In America, 600,000 people are homeless, and 200,000 of them are either schizophrenic or manic-depressive. I wonder what will happen to them in the wake of sensationalized reports of crimes committed by persons with a psychiatric history, such as Michael McDermott, described in Newsweek as a "depressed programmer" and "a little bit weird," Eric Harris and Dylan Klebold.

The chihuahuas, uniformed in blue serge with tiny brass buttons, guard and bark at the doors. No one is there. Grandma addresses the hissing registers where ghosts who want out could easily squeeze through the mesh. She lights incense in Buddha's lap because ghosts avoid smoke, especially sandalwood. She says coffins are lined with sandalwood, that burials and graveyards and funerary urns are a bad idea if you are a spirit, they are so hard to escape. Grandma hears phantoms screaming and crying, but she does not want them flitting about. She is not afraid, but she likes to keep a neat house. They are pranksters, and once they get out, you never can find anything: Stamps disappear, food is gone from the freezer, and money vanishes. I am here, a gaping 5-year-old because once again my mother has fled my father with her three small children and come to this place of featherbeds and sugar cookies, tarot cards, tea leaves and tales of levitation.

My grandmother's house is a gallery of paintings by her three children and her first husband. I have favorites, one by Mother of three charging horses, one by all of them of a black carriage resting on its shafts littered with falling leaves, and one by my grandfather, a curved canvas showing a place that might be the Arizona desert with real cacti and sand in the front. My grandmother plays the violin, my mother the piano. There are hats, gloves and rules of etiquette and deportment.

In the basement is an incinerator where a door opens to reveal the flames of hell. Stuff becomes ash. There is a mangle where Grandma presses clothing and linens, and vapor escapes in swirls, like long scarves. She comes at me with a hot curling iron. I smell my hair cooking into bananas, feel my skin shrivel in the heat. I picture the righteous coming for the outcast with hot tar and feathers, Puritans with their flaming torches and branding irons, Nazi ovens. I have already learned about all of them. I decide to cut my hair.

Grandma's food is boiled or pressure-cooked, and much of it is organ meat—brains, kidneys, liver, tongue—and mushy vegetables— turnips, parsnips, rutabagas. Steaming demons are everywhere, and I cling to her legs. I do not know what is safe. I do not know what to be afraid of.

Back home in the silver Airstream trailer, I have the upper bunk. I try to sleep, but evil clowns with glowing gums and polka-dot suits dance on my guardrail. They want to kill me. Even when I close my eyes, they are there. My mother says they are only moths, but she is wrong. She did not see the ghoulish octopus floating in my room that escaped from my dream to grope me with slimy tentacles. She never sees what I see, never believes what I tell her. No one does. This is 1954, four years after science discovers schizophrenia is not the result of bad upbringing, moral weakness or willful misbehavior, and a decade before my grandmother will commit suicide and my father will be diagnosed a paranoid schizophrenic.

When a family tree is riddled with madmen like a magnolia on a Civil War battlefield, it's hard to get a sense of where pathology ends and eccentricity begins. It's a shifting ground defined according to time, one diagnosis replaced by another, a pathology du jour. It's only because we do not believe in changelings anymore that we do not burn the bewitched. In the United States, 1 percent of the population is schizophrenic, their care costing $30 billion a year, and another 1 percent suffers mental illness.

My father enlisted and was attached to the 45th Infantry Brigade, the Thunderbirds, described by General George Patton as "one of the best, if not actually the best division in the history of American arms," the 180th Division, made famous by Bill Mauldin and Ernie Pyle. He shipped out to Oran, a city on the northwest coast of Africa, and spent the next two years at the front hiding in foxholes or engaged often in hand-to-hand combat from Sicily to Central Europe. His was the group to liberate Dachau. He was among those trapped on Anzio Beach. He suffered shell shock. One minute he was sitting next to another guy, and the next minute the guy had been replaced by a smoking crater littered with badges and bones. Post-traumatic stress disorder would not be an available diagnosis for another 30 years.

My father stayed on as an MP guarding relief trains in Germany. He is still haunted by visions of men disappearing in puffs of smoke, of hungry Fräuleins harvesting roots with bent forks. He came home a front-page hero, settled in Detroit, married, and bought a huge Mack-truck cab. He was a gypsy driver, a long-distance hauler responsible for loading and unloading tons of cargo. Sometimes at home he would make pulled taffy, and the muscles of his arms and neck, chest and back would pump like huge, hydraulic pistons while he stretched the sweet, white, chalky candy pliable in his powerful hands. After it dried into hard ropes, he'd crack it into pieces, slamming it down on the counter.

My mother and father told me the elderly man who gave kids money for candy was dangerous. I ignored their advice. They said I should steer clear of the fuming, bubbling sewage-treatment plant in the center of the park. I did not ignore that advice. I would dream that I fell over the Cyclone fence marked with Danger signs into the foul and foaming scum. Sometimes I dreamed I was abandoned in a car that plummeted down an embankment, hurling me to my death. I would feel myself falling through the bed night after night. I dreamed I was trapped on Detroit's busy train tracks and had to glue myself to the steel rails in order not to be killed by the Erie-Lackawanna. I had nightmares about being alive at the same time as dinosaurs; I was constantly in danger of being mashed. I was so small.

I was too young to know that my home, hazed with cigarette smoke, was atypical and dangerous. I would fall asleep to yelling and crying, demons and clowns, wake up to blue lights and scuffling and go to school. My mother, makeup hiding swollen eyes and a split lip, a grass-green anole chained to the pocket of her blouse, would appear at my classroom door. We would spend time with my grandmother and her ghosts.

No one ever said, "Your father is dangerous." To my young mind, if my father was not dangerous, and other things, like earthquakes, were menacing, I would see the clay mud of the trailer park crack and cup in the August heat and be terrified of falling into the great fissure and being lost forever. I would not walk there.

In summer in our bare feet and high-water pants, we looked like leftovers from the Great Depression. Like the Dalits, the Untouchables of India, whose very shadows and the winds that touch them are despised, we were shunned, always the new kids, never in the right clothes, begging for food. In third grade my teacher accused me of extorting food from a classmate; I was afraid I would be arrested. I stalked kids who had snack boxes of salted sunflower seeds. We were like the Musahars, the rat-eaters detested by other Untouchables. Everyone believes there is a bottom rung on the social ladder, and no one wants to be there.

We moved from trailer park to trailer park until we moved to another state. Gone were my grandmother's featherbeds, the Mack truck and my red-haired boyfriend who knew all the words to "Home on the Range." A fourth sibling was on the way. With my father's short list of references and extensive police record, it was a long and hungry time before he found work. I learned you can eat raw acorns without getting sick.

I played cowboys and Indians, hiked to a nearby pool, and smoked my first cigarette with the other kids. I was 10. I saw my father grab my little brother by the arm and fling him like a dead animal against a wall because he had lost a penny. I befriended the park owner's only child, a girl with long, dark braids and freckles, who played the accordion. I saw my father beat up her dad; I had run to them for help. His daughter and I hid under her bed while he barred the doorway. Like circus men who hammer tent pegs into parking-lot tar, my father pummeled him, breaking his glasses, his nose and cheekbone while we watched shards of glass and a few teeth slide toward us in a pool of blood. The park owner was sorry, but we had to move.

We spent the next winter with the trailer propped on cinder blocks next to the cellar hole where my uncle intended to build a house. Meanwhile he and his wife and his half-dozen kids lived in the garage where they probably would have stayed had it not burned down that winter. The heat from the fire melting the front of our trailer threatened to explode the propane tanks. My father turned off and disconnected the tanks, then rolled them to safety. We lived that winter without plumbing while my father cleared nearby land and in spring shoveled a well by hand, digging foxholes finally paying off. While we skated in the cellar hole, my fifth sibling was born.

The town had no high school or public transportation. There was a tuition plan, which a handful of eighth-graders took advantage of. We rode in and out of the city with our parents on the way to and from work, hanging out on the streets before school and in the shops after.

My freshman year I'm learning biology, Latin, geometry. My family has been in the same spot for three years. I have friends. We keep chickens for eggs. Rats move in. I baby-sit for a neighbor who raises broilers and knows what to do about rats. She gives me a yellow box of warfarin. It will make the rats' blood boil, and they will die. My father sees and seizes the poison, grabs my hair, and shakes the box over me. He's going to make me eat it. I don't really know why he doesn't. I don't know why he does any of the things he does, good or bad.

Back in Michigan my mother's mother has committed suicide, and her father is not well. My father's mother has died, and his father is in the county nursing home. We need a telephone, just in case. I meet a boy in the hallway at school and give him my number; he calls. I'm chatting on the phone, a white Princess that hangs in the kitchen. My father snaps the phone out of the wall and wraps the cold, white coils around my neck. It's hard to breathe between the welts.

I'm old enough to drink coffee. I fetch the percolator. My father grips it, splashing me with boiling coffee that stains my clothes and blisters my skin. He threatens to pour the whole pot over me. I feel myself split like Hydra, one part wanting to shrivel into oblivion, the other to grow into a powerful monster. I'm fascinated by Siamese twins, and I really don't care anymore about kingdom and phylum and the sums of angles and the conjugation of verbs. The air around me shimmers with toxic fumes; the septic backs up into the trailer and everything stinks. I have seen the silver revolver. I have seen the Smith & Wesson. Pamela Mason's body has been found behind a neighbor's house, and a friend of my father's has been stopped with a bloody hunting knife in the glove compartment of his car after the murder of Sandra Valarde. I know teen-agers can die deliberate, sudden, violent deaths.

The dawn of my 16th birthday I tell my father I don't want to go to school. I walk to a police station in the morning and run through the woods to the home of the neighbors in the evening, escaping my father and his deer rifle. He is arrested, tried, found incompetent, and sentenced to the maximum-security section of the state mental hospital. It's as quick as that.

I'm learning first hand about discrimination. It settles like atomic dust on the families of troublesome people. In Early Ages, Mrs. R. assigns each student a book, most a couple of hundred pages long. She assigns me a fat, two-volume set, then complains my handwriting on the report is too small. She gives me a failing grade. She does the same thing to Shirley J., whose brother, Lance, is a well-known local lunatic. Mrs. R. singles us out, asking impossible questions — Who was the Supreme Padishah of Persia in the 11th century? What river flows from the Arno to the sea? What is written on the 12th scroll of the Apocrypha? She smirks when we cannot answer. The only thing Shirley and I share is our notorious relatives, seen on the 6 o'clock news and discussed in the evening edition.

Some of my family visit la-la-land daily. Those who learn the secret of keeping quiet pass as normal. Shhh. When people read about the Jeffrey Dahmers of the world, they are repulsed and retreat, leaving their care to the courts, the state, the prisoners, but somewhere are relatives who hide and perhaps change their names to pass inconspicuously. Their history is baggage. The trick is to make the baggage history.

Spinach with roasted goat cheese and red peppers, pumpkin soup and chocolate paté. My husband and I are lunching with another couple we have only recently met. We are all college-educated liberals, older. Conversation wanders around the usual topics of politics, education, how you met your spouse, then ambles into the dangerous turf I prefer to avoid. I'm asked about my parents. At my age most people don't go there, and I have developed answers that satisfy without exposing too much, a trick I learned long ago at another restaurant. The man whose birthday we were celebrating sat at the head of the table, and the group discussed what parents did for a living. Astrophysicist, neurosurgeon, diplomat.

By this time I had outlived the shame of my father's incarceration, my stepfather's reputation as a pervert and the experience of being a social pariah, as welcome with my holey socks and hand-me-downs as a leper ringing her bells. "He's an engineer." The word *engineer* falls over a conversation like a blanket over a birdcage. After a moment of silence, the group sputtered on to another topic. I had succeeded in passing as normal.

What do you say when a date asks about your family? Daddy's had enough electroshock therapy they may let him out soon. My stepfather is a 7-foot pedophile. Mother is in the hospital having either another baby or another "nervous breakdown," a diagnosis that no longer exists. You just keep quiet, learn the lingo of the successful in society, and distance yourself as rapidly as possible. Sometimes I feel like an orphan with amnesia, moving from the land of the insane to the land of the sane, leaving behind fatherland and mother tongue.

I wonder about the man with the iguana, wonder who of the people walking by has been found in a Dumpster, a closet or reeds by the river. I wonder if anyone would recognize a Moses today. I look at the homeless men asleep under the overpass, hitching rides, pedaling bicycles, all they possess balanced on the handlebars, and wonder what to say, what to do. Do they strangle canaries with their bare hands because they warn too late of bad air and ozone? My father does. He can barely eat because all the food is poison, all the water tainted. He smokes and drinks from a paper bag and gets lost in his dream world. He no longer cares if anyone believes him or that no one is listening. There's a crowd in his head, and he's still trying to sort out the good guys from the bad. His mood swings are swift, unexpected and dangerous. His life crashes to a halt daily. All his delusions are vivid and smell of crankcase oil and spilled wine. The noises made by the wind and cars and dishes have secret, intended meanings.

Until the 1960s schizophrenics were locked up, shocked and lobotomized into oblivion. Now they are left to the asylum of poverty, anonymous and forgotten. My uncle searches for another brother in the Bowery and learns the hard way that "bums" recognize and look out for each other.

Diversity implies immigrants, foreigners who come with their children and parents, ocarinas and mandolins, colorful clothes and peculiar foods. There is little difference between growing up in a deranged family and being an immigrant, but the nostalgia we feel exists in our imaginations, not our memories. There are no block parties, no celebrations of Day of the Demented, no parades, no marches for pride, no books, "Psychotic Like Me," no culture of the insane.

It is not interesting or politically correct to mention that most murders are committed by white, heterosexual males with no history of mental illness. Reading a Justice Department report in reverse, 96 percent of the murders committed in 1998 were committed by people with no history of mental illness. According to a report published in 1990, 90 percent of the people who physically assaulted another person were not mentally ill. Two recent articles, one published in Lancet and the other in Science News, cite studies that reveal a steady decline in the number of homicides committed by the mentally ill, and that the mentally ill, unless they abuse drugs or alcohol, are no more likely to commit a violent crime than anyone else. Both the general population and the population of persons with a major mental illness see an increase, three- and fourfold, in violent behavior if they abuse drugs or alcohol. Finding ways to curb substance abuse would do more to eliminate crime than eliminating the mentally ill. After sensationalized events such as the Columbine High School or Wakefield, Mass., murders, there is a tidal wave of interest and outrage, scapegoating aimed at people with a history of mental illness.

In 1907 Indiana passed the first mandatory sterilization law against criminals, idiots, rapists and imbeciles; by 1980, 30 states had adopted mandatory sterilization. In 1912 the first International Congress of Eugenics took place in London—not Berlin—and psychologist Henry Goddard determined, after administering IQ tests to immigrants arriving at Ellis Island, that the majority of Jews, Hungarians, Italians and Russians were feebleminded. In 1922 H.H. Laughlin, expert eugenics agent to the U.S. House of Representatives Committee on Immigration and Naturalization, listed the following people for mandatory sterilization: the feebleminded, insane, criminalistic, diseased, deformed and dependent.

In 1935 Dr. Alexis Carrel, a French-American Nobel Prize–winner, wondered why society did not dispose of criminals and the insane in an economical way; he suggested gas-filled euthanasia chambers. In 1937 Professor Ernest A. Hooten of Harvard stated for the New York Times, "I think that a biological purge is the essential prerequisite for a social and spiritual salvation." By 1945, according to the AMA, 42,000 people were sterilized in the United States between 1941 and 1943.

In 1970 psychologist James V. McConnell, concerned only with the individual's economic contribution to modern industrial society, said in Psychology Today, "We should reshape society so that we all would be trained from birth to want to do what society wants us to do." In 1979 the Repository for Germinal Choice in Escondido, Calif., began collecting elite semen from Nobel Prize–winners and others; in 1982 the first baby from this sperm bank was born.

On any given day, 40 percent of the mentally ill are untreated. Most are delusional, harmless oddballs, highly creative, whether believing the hum of the phone wires is Napoleon trying to speak to them or that they are the true heirs to the thrones of England or Spain or that they are writing some of the world's finest literature. A few, like my father, are dangerous. Since de-institutionalization began in the 1960s, 90 percent of hospital psychiatric beds have been eliminated. Instead of an increase in services for the mentally ill, there has been an increase in suicide, incarceration and assignment to nursing homes where Medicare and Medicaid pick up the bill. One third of the nation's 600,000 homeless people are schizophrenic or manic-depressive, and a similar number are in jail for misdemeanors. According to the Southern Poverty Law Report, 16 percent of the prisoners in the United States have serious mental illness; many remain untreated. After an eight-year court battle, Alabama officials agreed to comply with the law and provide for the needs of mentally ill inmates, who until September of last year, were simply stripped and locked in isolation cells.

In this age of memoir, this age of vicarious living, it is hip to have been disadvantaged, to rise not only from poverty but also from hideous circumstance—unless it involves mental illness. Those with a psychiatric history remain the untouchables of our society, the ones singled out in news reports. We ignore or make fun of or steer clear of the dysfunctional who roam parking lots, sleep in doorways, or bum cigarettes until there is an incident and the cant of modern culture cries out for punishment—the death sentence, lobotomies, electroshock, eugenics—to eliminate the uncomfortable nuance of difference, to fine-tune society.

In 1892 Gottlieb Burkhardt performed leucotomies on six patients with a history of hallucination and agitation. Two of them died. Leucotomies did not catch on until 1936, when Dr. Moniz of Portugal promoted the surgery. He retired four years later after being shot and paralyzed by one of his ex-patients; in 1955 he was beaten to death by another. That same year Drs. Freeman and Watts standardized the procedure and introduced the word *lobotomy*.

Dr. Freeman demonstrated lobotomies at the University of Virginia in 1948. He plunged the ice-pick-like instrument in through the eye socket, lifted the eyelid to slide it over the eyeball, then stabbed it in suddenly and moved it from side to side to sever the prefrontal lobe, a procedure so ghastly that seasoned surgeons like Dr. Watts could not stand the sight of it. Dr. Freeman had each operation photographed with the instrument in place.

After World War II, asylums filled with mental cases, thanks to morphine, plasma and penicillin at the front. In the years between 1945 and 1965, 50,000 lobotomies were performed in the United States. Although Dr. Moniz won the 1949 Nobel Prize, scientific evidence for the benefit of the surgery did not develop. One third of the lobotomized patients improved, one third remained the same, and one third became worse, like Phineas Gage, a 19th-century railroad foreman. He suffered an accidental lobotomy when a spike with which he was tamping dynamite was blown backward through his skull. Although he survived, he became a notorious, antisocial psychotic. Researchers reported in Archives of General Psychiatry that based on MRI scans of their brains, a group of men with antisocial personality disorders, a condition characterized by violence, had smaller prefrontal cortexes than a control group, further proving lobotomies counter-intuitive.

My father was not lobotomized, but he did receive electroshock treatments in the state mental hospital. In ancient times, electric eels, skates, rays and chimeras were used to mediate mental illness. In 1938 Ugo Cerletti observed slaughterhouse workers shocking pigs to death instead of bludgeoning them on the head. After destroying numerous dogs while experimenting, Cerletti began treating schizophrenic patients with jolts of electricity. His first subject was a homeless man speaking gibberish. He shocked the man several times until he cried out to stop or it would kill him.

My father was in the state hospital at the same time the real Sylvia Plath and the fictional McMurphy in Ken Kesey's 1962 novel, "One Flew Over the Cuckoo's Nest," underwent electroshock therapy. In the novel a character, Harding, says of the treatments, "The thing is, no one ever wants another one." Later Harding tells McMurphy not to worry because "It's almost out of vogue and only used in extreme cases nothing else seems to reach, like lobotomy."

Doctors have changed the name to *electroconvulsive therapy* and use sedatives and muscle relaxants so patients do not remember what happened and are less likely to suffer broken bones. Up to 30 shocks may be given to treat a patient. In Texas, the only state to keep track of shock-therapy statistics, there is a 360 percent increase in ECT treatments for people who are 65 as compared to those who are 64, the difference being that Medicare and Medicaid will pay for it.

We accept as human, as we should, the elephant man, the hydro-cephalic, the thalidomide-damaged, the hideous and different, and reserve our jokes and hatred for the mentally ill. By the time I went to college, an Ivy League school, I had learned to keep my mouth shut. Shhh. I listened to the nature-nurture debate, read that people who are neglected or exposed to traumatic events as children were being set up for problems later. I vowed that with my genetic overload, I would never have children because I was doomed to be a bad and dangerous parent. Years later I became more optimistic. My kids have inherited creativity—think Dali, think Hunter S. Thompson, Ralph Steadman, Edward Gory, think Florida ballot, think faulty wiring— but they have learned to turn this to their advantage. They think their grandpa is weird, but they are not afraid of him. They listen to his rants, and they are glad when he brings gifts, spaghetti sauce he has made, a microscope, a treasure box of old coins. They recognize his complex history, appreciate the contributions he has made, laugh at his terrible puns.

My father lives with an overweight beagle in a small apartment on a quiet street. There is a yard spilling down to the river where he plants a garden of tomatoes, peppers and summer squash, which he shares. He has a white SUV but rarely goes anywhere. Whether we visit or talk by phone, phrases catch in his verbal tornado: "tapped phone lines," "drop cement blocks on their head," "matzoh-ball soup," "friggin' bastards," "Sewer Crates" (Socrates).

Imagination and mania both possess a fine-tuned, overly sensitive nervous system, disinhibition, ragged clothes or angel wings, palaver or philosophy, scatology or foul language, and hypomania, an ability for absorption associated with superior powers of concentration, especially pronounced among writers, especially poets. Examples are Robert Lowell, Randall Jarrell and Theodore Roethke, who could live with their manias and hypomanias; and Sylvia Plath, John Berryman and Anne Sexton, who could not. Would we cross the street if we saw them coming, close the door if they knocked?

People touched by manic fire are sharing their stories. Chris Marrou, news anchor for KENS-TV in San Antonio, Texas, and a sufferer of anxiety attacks, said in a Newsweek column that he tried to tough it out, that "being a macho Texan," he "didn't need no stinkin' pills" until he could no longer function without intervention. Kay Redfield Jamison, professor of medicine, author of "An Unquiet Mind" and a manic-depressive, cautions, "Being open is the sort of thing that I advise people to think very long and hard about." Greg Bottoms, brother of a schizophrenic and author of "Angelhead: My Brother's Descent Into Madness," says, "Our true stories... are often the ones that we wish most to forget—a kind of apocrypha from our lives that we keep secret and attempt to excise from the narrative of the self." They are opening doors for Iguana Don.

Patricia L. Frisella is an award-winning poet living in rural New Hampshire. She graduated from Mount Holyoke College in 1972 with a bachelor's degree in Spanish existentialist literature. Last Veterans Day, Frisella's father was awarded the Bronze Star and other medals for his service during World War II.

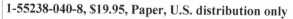

A HANDS-ON, HEARTFELT GUIDE *for* AFRICAN AMERICAN WRITERS

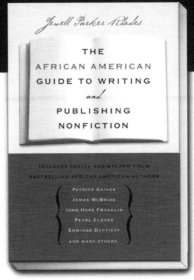

Expressly addressing the needs of budding African American authors of memoirs, autobiographies, and personal essays, this carefully crafted guide treats the entire writing experience, showing how to:

- FIND AND RESEARCH SUBJECTS
- EXPLORE THE LEGACY OF YOUR LITERARY ANCESTORS
- PLUMB MEMORIES AND EXPERIENCES FOR MATERIAL
- KNOW WHEN TO REVISE AND WHEN TO LET GO

Including excerpts from such greats as Maya Angelou and inspirational wisdom from James McBride, Patrice Gaines, Edwidge Danticat, and more, this is required reading for any aspiring author.

Available wherever books are sold. Just ask. www.broadwaybooks.com

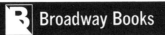
Broadway Books

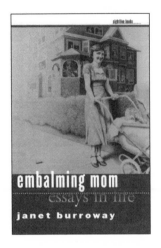
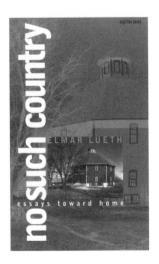